The Best EUROPEAN TRAVEL TIPS

by John Whitman

Meadowbrook Press
Wayzata, MN 55391

Library of Congress Cataloging in Publication Data

Whitman, John.
    The Best European Travel Tips.

    (The Best Tips Series)
    Includes index.
    1. Europe—Description and travel—1971—
—Guide-book. I. Title.
D909.W536   914'.04558   80-11765
ISBN 0-915658-21-6

Copyright © 1980 by John Whitman

First printing March, 1980

Printed in the United States of America.

CONTENTS

Note use Canadian not American observes 1st 27yrs old

MAPS AND CHARTS

Part I: Preparations

TRAVEL DOCUMENTS

You'll need certain documents to travel freely through Europe or to avoid potential problems. Here are some tips to make the whole process of getting these documents less costly and more enjoyable.

PASSPORTS

If you are planning a trip to Europe, you must obtain a passport. If you already have one, check the expiration date on p. 2 to see whether the passport will be valid for the entire length of your trip. If it will expire during your stay in Europe, you must apply for a new one.

Kinds of passports

- Each person in your party should have an individual passport. Although it is legal and less expensive for a couple or a family to travel on a single, group passport, the freedom and flexibility allowed by having individual passports is worth the extra thirteen dollars per person.

- If you plan to travel in Eastern Europe, ask for the special forty-eight-page passport when you apply. It costs no more than the standard document and provides added space for the visas you will need (see p. 12).

When to apply for a passport

- If you intend to travel to Western Europe only, apply for a passport three months before your trip. (Traveling in Eastern Europe is more complicated, and you should start the application process as long as six months before you want to leave: see p. 12.)

- In an emergency you can obtain a passport in a few hours, at a substantial fee. This service is not available to the jet setter who decides on a whim to get a passport overnight; it is reserved for emergencies only!

Applying for a first passport

- To get your first passport, you must apply in person at the appropriate agency. So must all members of your family who plan to carry individual passports and who are twelve years of age or older. Younger children need not appear in person.

- Couples must appear together if they want a joint passport, as must all family members sixteen years old and older if they are applying for a single passport for the group.

- The passport agency is listed in your telephone directory under U.S. Government Offices. If there is no passport agency in your town, the service may be handled at a federal, state, or probate courthouse or at a designated post office. Call the listed number for hours.

- Be sure to ask the clerk about the least busy hours to come in and apply for a passport.

What to bring when you apply

Passport application You will need to fill out a passport application in person at the appropriate passport agency.

Proof of U.S. citizenship For proof of U.S. citizenship, come armed with a birth certificate or certified copy (look for a raised seal imprinted on the copy) or with a certificate of naturalization or citizenship. If you don't have any of these, you can get by with certificates of baptism or circumcision; hospital birth records; documentary evidence from census, school, or insurance companies; or affidavits. No proof, no passport!

Proof of identity If you're known to the clerk or if you have a certificate of naturalization or citizenship, that's all the proof of identity you'll need. Otherwise you must produce a valid driver's license, a government identification card or pass, or a witness. The witness must have valid identification (passport, driver's license, government pass, or certificate of naturalization or citizenship) and must have known you for at least two years. All identification must bear signatures and photos.

Two passport photos You'll need two passport photos, taken within the last six months. Each should be signed on the front, along the left-hand edge. Note that photos taken in a photomat machine will not be acceptable. Passport photos must be 2½ by 2½ inches at the smallest and no larger than 3 by 3 inches. They should be clear, front-view shots of your head and shoulders only, taken against a white background. No hats or sunglasses allowed! Prints must be on thin, nonglossy paper. Photos can be either in color or in black and white.

Passport photos

- If you are applying for a group (couple or family) passport, bring along a group photograph. It's less expensive than using individual photos and causes fewer delays in passport processing. (Note again that I suggest having individual passports!)

- Many agencies issuing passports now offer a passport photo service as well. Be sure to call ahead to see whether such a service is available in your area. Ask what the fee will be and the cost of **extra** prints. Then call several passport photo studios listed under the same title in the yellow pages as well as the local branch of the American Automobile Association (AAA) for cost comparison. A separate trip might save you several dollars if you're so inclined.

- You will need two photos for your passport. You should always carry two spare copies for emergencies. And you will need extra photos for visas (see p. 12).

Passport fees

- You will be charged a ten-dollar passport fee and a three-dollar execution fee for each passport. Only major passport agencies will take cash. In other places you'll pay with a bank draft, money order, or check (personal, traveler's, certified, or cashier's).

- Call ahead to see how the office wants the payment to be made: this may well save you from a frustrating experience. "What do you mean, you won't take thirteen dollars in cash?" You have been warned!

Applying if you have had a passport before

- If you have had a passport during the last eight years and don't intend to make a change (such as adding a member of your family), apply for your new passport by mail. This will save you a trip and a three-dollar execution fee.

- Call the nearest passport agency and ask them to send you Passport Office Form DSP-82, "Application for Passport by Mail." When this form arrives in the mail, fill it out, sign, and date it. Attach your old passport, two up-to-date passport photos signed on the front along the left-hand edge, and a check or money order for ten dollars to cover the passport fee.

- If your name has changed, be sure to include the original or a certified copy of your marriage certificate, or of the change-of-name papers, when making an application by mail.

- Be sure to send the passport by registered mail and hold on to the receipt until the new passport arrives.

- **A special note:** if you were under eighteen when you

applied for your old passport, you'll have to apply for the new one in person.

- Naturally, you can always apply for a passport in person if you prefer. But in that case you must pay the three-dollar execution fee.

Protecting yourself and your passport

- When your passport arrives in the mail, check it for correctness before signing it on p. 2. If there is an error in any of the information, you must return the passport to have it corrected. Fill in the information on the inside front cover (your address in the United States, your foreign address, and a person to contact in case of emergency). This is the only information you can change at a later date without invalidating the document. Never write in, alter, or mutilate any portion of the passport, as this would make it invalid.

- Make two photocopies of the information on pp. 2 and 3. On both photocopies, write your passport number, which is perforated through the front cover and first few pages. These photocopies will be **invaluable** if your passport is lost or stolen. File one of the photocopies in a safe place and take the other with you to Europe. Don't carry it with your passport!

If you lose your passport in the United States

- If your passport is lost or stolen in the United States, contact the Passport Office, Department of State, Washington, DC 20524 **immediately.** You'll need information which you've recorded on a photocopy of the original passport.

VISAS

Visas are special notations and stamps, added to your passport by officials of foreign countries, which allow you to enter and leave these countries. Western European countries do not require visas except for long-term stays (over three months). On the other hand, Eastern European countries do demand visas, even for short stays.

Where to get visas

- Obtain all visas before going to Europe. Visa information is outlined in a government leaflet entitled **Visa Requirements of Foreign Governments** (Passport Office Publication M-264). You can get the leaflet from most passport agencies. This will tell you what countries require visas. You'll then have to write the embassy or consulate of the foreign country to get a visa application form with information on fees and procedure. You'll generally have to send passport photos along with a completed application and payment for the service.

- You will have to mail the passport along with the application, so that it can be stamped. Be sure to use registered mail and keep the receipt until your passport has been returned.

- Always apply for visas at the foreign embassy or consulate in your city or the city nearest you. Most embassies and consulates are located in New York, Chicago, San Francisco, and Washington, DC. You'll find their addresses in individual city directories or in the **Congressional Directory**, found in most major libraries.

- If you intend to travel to areas requiring visas, allow an extra three to six weeks for each necessary visa. Obtaining visas can be a long—disturbingly long—process. You may want to start the process months ahead of your planned trip!

MEDICAL DOCUMENTS

For more medical information, be sure to read the section on what to do about problems as they come up in Europe. This is outlined in detail starting on p. 187.

International Certificates of Vaccination

At one time everyone traveling to Europe was required to show proof of smallpox vaccination. Since smallpox has been officially eradicated, such proof is no longer necessary. The proof consisted of a doctor's signature in what was called a "yellow card." These yellow cards are still available and are technically called **International Certificates of Vaccination.**

Although yellow cards are no longer necessary for travel to Europe, it doesn't hurt to have one. By having all your immunizations listed in this official document, you have an accurate record of them. In the case of an unusual outbreak of a specific disease you can be immunized abroad and have that noted in the yellow card. This will allow you to cross the border into and out of a "disease zone." Such an occurrence is rare, but it does happen—particularly in the case of cholera.

Most passport agencies have copies of the yellow card, which is given out free of charge.

Medical preparations for travel

- Before going on a trip, see both a doctor and a dentist for a quick checkup. Have your doctor fill out the yellow card with a complete history of your immunizations. He may suggest some new ones, depending upon the areas you intend to visit. Never ask travel agents for information on health matters, since they're generally behind on current problems. Check with a public health office, the best being state headquarters where bulletins are kept up to date on disease outbreaks worldwide.

- For useful, current bulletins on disease, contact the Center for Disease Control, Atlanta, GA 30333. The center issues warnings on outbreaks of hepatitis (preventable on a short-term basis by a shot of gamma globulin) and giardiasis, a parasitic infection causing cramps and stomach problems (common in Leningrad).

- Nowadays you need take only those immunizations that are really necessary. Typhoid and cholera vaccinations are rarely recommended any longer and give only short-term protection at best.

- If a public health officer or your doctor recommends vaccinations, be sure to get them well ahead of your planned trip. You want to avoid any possible side effects during the trip itself.

- Note that it's often possible to get free vaccinations at public clinics. Call your local health department to see whether such a service is available in your area.

- Get prescriptions from your doctor to cover common travel health problems: anxiety, diarrhea, constipation, and insomnia. You may wish to have him prescribe a few sleeping pills for flights across the Atlantic.

Chronic health problems

- If you have a chronic health problem, take with you all the drugs you'll need for the entire trip and include enough to cover a week or two in case of an unexpected extended stay.

- Be sure to carry the prescription with you, so as to avoid hassles when crossing borders. And ask your doctor for the generic name of each drug, since brand names will differ in foreign countries.

- Never put drugs into luggage that will be checked onto the plane at the airport. Carry all drugs with you in your hand luggage.

- Two useful organizations to know about if you have a chronic illness or health problem: International Association for Medical Assistance to Travelers, 350 Fifth Avenue, Suite 5620, New York, NY 10001, (212) 279-6465; and Intermedic, 777 Third Avenue, New York, NY 10017, (212) 486-8974.

Diabetics

- Diabetics should read the special section on p. 188 which outlines appropriate precautions under these circumstances. Recommended identification: a necklace or bracelet with one of the symbols used by Medic Alert (see below).

Medic Alert

Medic Alert Foundation International is a worldwide organization with over a million members. It provides useful medical tags for people with specific medical problems, such as allergies to penicillin, sulfa drugs, anesthetics, and pain killers; cardiovascular disease; diabetes; epilepsy; and so on. The tag contains an identification number, the medical information, and a toll-free telephone number for emergencies. Medic Alert also provides you with a medical information card to put in your wallet. The cost of lifetime membership varies with the style of necklace or bracelet chosen.

- Contact Medic Alert, P.O. Box 1009, Turlock, CA 95380, or one of the regional offices: 840 North Lake Shore Drive, Chicago, IL 60611; 3 East 54th Street, New York NY 10022; 600 Courtland Street, Orlando, FL 32804; 445 East Second South, Salt Lake City, UT 84111.

Guide to U.S. Certified Doctors Abroad

A new **Guide to U.S. Certified Doctors Abroad** is available to American Express Cardmembers only. It contains information on 3,500 physicians in 120 foreign countries and is available for three dollars from Customer Service, American Express Company, Church Street Station, New York, NY 10008.

INTERNATIONAL DRIVER'S LICENSE

If you plan to drive at all in Europe, you should get an International Driver's License. It's required in most countries, helps you avoid hassles with the police, and occasionally gets you out of a fine.

How to get licensed

- To get a license, you must be eighteen years of age or older and you must hold a valid driver's license.

- You can get a license from the local branch of the American Automobile Asssociation (AAA) without being a member.

- You'll need two photomat photos; keep the extras. Make sure they are as similar to your passport photos as possible. Note that many branches of AAA offer a photo service, but the cost is higher than in photomats.

- You'll be asked to sign the photos.

- You may have to return or have the license sent to you. Such a license is not valid until you sign it. It's good for one year from its issue date.

Stick shifts

- If you don't know how to operate a stick shift, you should learn. Even if you reserve a car with automatic shift, there's no guarantee that you'll get one. Furthermore, in an emergency you should be able to drive any car that's available. A competent driving instructor can teach you how to use a stick shift in six hours or less —from the basics to starting on a ninety-degree incline.

INTERNATIONAL STUDENT IDENTIFICATION CARD

If you're a full-time student under the age of thirty, get an International Student Identification Card! It will bring reductions on inter-European charter flights (save 75 percent); on all forms of transportation; in hotels and hostels; at museums, movies, galleries, and special events; and in many shops. **This card can save you hundreds of dollars.**

To get a card

- You'll need two photomat photos (similar to the passport pose), a copy of your fee statement as proof of full-time student status, and a check for three dollars made out to CIEE (Council on International Educational Exchange), 205 East 42nd Street, New York, NY 10017; or 312 Sutter Street, San Francisco, CA 94108.

- Or you may be able to get a card from the student office of a local university. This would be a faster way of getting the card, since it may take three or four weeks from CIEE.

CHECKS AND CREDIT CARDS

Each year, more than a million travelers lose cash in Europe due to theft and negligence. For this reason, you should rely on traveler's checks as a way of carrying money throughout Europe, and you can extend your purchasing power by using credit.

Traveler's checks

- Traveler's checks are available from American Express,

Bank of America, Barclay's Bank, Citibank, Thomas Cook, and many other institutions.

- Normally, you'll pay a 1 percent service fee when buying these checks.

Fee-free traveler's checks

Offers come and go, but if you'll look around, you'll find traveler's checks that you can buy without paying the 1 percent fee. It's worth the effort.

- If you are a member of the American Automobile Association (AAA), you can buy Thomas Cook traveler's checks without paying the 1 percent service fee. You must pay for them with cash, cashier's check, or bank money order. No personal checks will be accepted.

- If you have a Diners Club International (Amoco) card, you can get $750 worth of Thomas Cook traveler's checks free of any service charge every fourteen days with a personal check, plus additional checks free of service charge when you pay with cash. Just show your card when purchasing them.

- Many banks offer special account customers free traveler's checks.

- In New York, you can get Barclay's traveler's checks free of any service fee when you pay with a cashier's check or bank money order—even if you're from out of state.

When you buy traveler's checks

- Make sure to count them, since they're usually sold in packets containing a specific amount in specific denominations. Very rarely will a check be missing, but it doesn't hurt to be sure.

- Be sure to sign them as instructed. If you lose an unsigned check, it's gone forever.

- Couples should carry individual checks. Otherwise, you'll both have to be present at foreign banks to cash them—ridiculous!

- Note numbers on a separate sheet just in case you lose them.

- Get checks of varying denominations to avoid the currency exchange rip-off. You only want to exchange the amount of money you really need.

- Buy all traveler's checks in the United States. If you buy them in Europe, your currency will go through two exchanges before being converted into checks. You might lose 5 percent of your money just on the exchange, not to mention paying an added 1 percent service fee.

Letters of credit, bank money orders, or cashier's checks

- You may have heard of letters of credit. Well, forget them. Banks abroad rarely honor them—without horrendous arguments. Do not attempt to travel with letters of credit!
- The same goes for bank money orders and cashier's checks. Although perfectly legitimate, they're next to impossible to cash. Your time is too valuable to waste in dismal corridors of foreign banks.

Personal checks

- You may not believe it, but it is a good idea to take some personal checks with you. Bring about half a dozen. You'll be surprised at the hotels, restaurants, and shops that will take them. Use them only for big-bill items.

Credit cards

- Since you can use credit cards in thousands of European hotels, restaurants, and shops, why not take them with you—just in case?
- When you use credit cards, you have excellent records of your expenses for business purposes.
- You can get cash in emergencies from major card companies.
- You can use mail service free of charge.
- When using credit cards abroad, ask the restaurant, hotel, or shop to convert the amount of the total bill into an equivalent dollar figure. Ask the clerk to write the dollar figure on the slip. This is the easiest way to keep track of your total expenses, and neither you nor the credit card company will be forced to convert bills into dollar figures at a later date. Most places will agree to do this.

INSURANCE

If you carry any insurance at all, it will probably cover your trip to Europe. Exceptions to this general rule, and additional information on the subject, are detailed below.

Life insurance

- If you already carry a reasonable amount of life insurance, you won't need any extra for a vacation. The so-called **flight insurance** is basically a rip-off, making the insurance companies millions of dollars.

- Note that flying is—statistically—incredibly safe.

- Call your agent to find out whether your policy is written with a double-indemnity clause for accidental death.

- You may have extra coverage already through AAA or any travel clubs to which you belong. Call them and inquire.

Health insurance

- Check with your insurance company to make sure you will be covered wherever you intend to travel. (Most health insurance policies do cover you worldwide.)

- Carry your insurance card, your agent's telephone number, and your insurance company's telephone number when you travel. In some European countries, you will be covered, at least partially, by national health insurance; in most countries, however, you'll have to pay for all services—which is a good reason to have that information at hand.

Baggage insurance

- Read your homeowner's policy. In most instances, it will cover your baggage up to a value of $1,000.

- If you must bring along any expensive articles, such as furs, jewelry, and cameras, pay a small fee to have a **personal articles floater** added to your policy—or, better yet, leave all expensive articles at home!

- Find out whether your policy covers new purchases made abroad under a floater for a thirty- to ninety-day grace period.

- If you don't have a homeowner's policy, buy special baggage insurance, which is available from most insurance companies and can be obtained directly from the airline at check-in time.

- Do some comparison shopping over the phone to come up with the least expensive coverage. Don't assume the costs will be comparable.

- To protect yourself, keep a list of all the clothes and personal belongings packed in each bag. Also note the honest value of each article.

- Note that if any of your bags are lost or damaged during the flight, the airline will reimburse you up to a reasonable amount (see p. 93).

Home insurance

- Since your home may not be covered if you are away for more than thirty days, check with your agent for advice if you plan an extended trip.

Trip cancellation insurance

- Some flights are sold only on a restricted basis and have stiff cancellation charges. If you must cancel the flight because of an emergency—such as illness or death in the immediate family—trip cancellation insurance can remove the sting.

- Note that this insurance is not valid when the illness has been in existence during the previous year.

Rain insurance

- A whimsical concept, this insurance pays you if you run into rainy days that in theory spoil a trip to Europe. It has so many exclusions for such a high price that it's a blatant rip-off.

DOCUMENTS FOR A TRUSTED FRIEND

Following is a list of things you should leave with a trusted friend. Although your trip may go without a hitch, this simple precaution could save you an incredible amount of trouble and time.

Itinerary Come as close to places and dates as possible. Leave exact mailing addresses (see advice on mail, p. 166).

List of traveler's check numbers You should carry a list of these numbers, but it's a very good idea to leave a duplicate list at home—just in case you lose everything, including the duplicate list.

Numbers of credit cards You should carry a list of these numbers as well and, once again, you should leave a duplicate list with a friend.

Number, date, and place of issue of passport You should memorize this information as soon as you get the passport. You'll need it when checking in at hotels. If you lose a passport, it will be essential information.

Airline ticket numbers, date and place of issue If you want to get reimbursed for lost or stolen tickets with a minimum of hassle, have these numbers readily available.

2
ITINERARIES

Determining what countries you'll visit and what spots in each country you'll see is the most obvious step in planning your itinerary. The "Best of Europe" chart in the appendix lists many places you'll want to consider, and this chapter will give you many hints for planning the best trip you can have.

WHERE TO GO

You may know from the start where you want to go; you may be open to any suggestion. Either way, the more care you take in picking places to go the more fun you'll have abroad.

Basic considerations

- If you and any potential travel partner can't agree on where to go, plan to travel independently. You can still arrange to meet to do the things you **can** agree on during your trips.

- If you'll be traveling with kids, give them some say about where to go. They'll be much better travelers for it.

- If **money** is a major consideration in your plans, you may wish to restrict your itinerary to southern Europe. The least expensive countries to travel in are Greece, Italy, Portugal, and Spain. Austria, Belgium, Luxembourg, Netherlands and Norway are moderately expensive. Denmark, Finland, France, Germany, Sweden and Switzerland are expensive.

- If **time** is a problem, plan your trip to the minute. If you've only got a week, you don't want to waste even an hour.

- And if your own **energy** is limited, save it by joining a tour going to the places you want to see.

Fine-tuning your choices

- Go to the library to browse in travel books and magazines (see p. 22) so you have an idea of the possibilities.

- Look as well at newspaper travel sections, especially the **New York Times** Sunday travel sections, for more up-to-date news of attractions.

- Try to get a copy of papers from cities you might visit in Europe (newsstands and libraries may have them). Check out concerts, plays, and sporting events you may want to attend.

SOURCES OF INFORMATION

The more you know, the better you'll plan; the better you plan, the more fun you'll have on your trip. The information you can get from these sources will make you a travel expert, whether or not you combine your reading with extensive travel.

Magazines and Reports

Recommended Magazines

- **Gourmet**   (for its fine restaurant recommendations)
- **Travel and Leisure**   (for general travel hints)

Recommended Travel Reports

- **Association of Informed Travelers,** 115 Brand Road, Salem, VA 24153
- **Great Expeditions,** Box 46499, Vancouver, BC, Canada V6R 4G7
- **Joyer Travel Report,** 7315 Wisconsin Avenue, Suite 1200 North, Bethesda, MD 20014
- **Passport,** 20 North Wacker Drive, Chicago, IL 60606
- **Travel Advisor,** 15 Park Place, Suite 2, Bronxville, NY 10708
- **Travel Letter for Corporate Executives,** Corpcom Services, Inc., 112 East 31st Street, New York, NY 10016
- **Travel Smart,** Communications House, 40 Beechdale Road, (Dobbs Ferry), New York, NY 10522
- To find out which one of these suits your personality, write to several of them and ask for a sample copy, for which there will be a small charge.

Books—Elementary and Advanced

Good Travel Books

- **Fielding**   (nonbudget travel)
- **Fodor**   (good general guides)
- **Frommer**   (budget travel)
- **Uncommon Guide to Europe**   (off the beaten path)
- **Egon Ronay**   (good on Great Britain)
- **Michelin Red Guides**   (excellent hotel and restaurant ratings)
- **Blue Guides**   (minutely detailed information for experts)
- **Eurail Guide**   (for train travel)

Specialized Books for the Travel Trade

- Plan your own itinerary (if you are so inclined) by using these specialized books: **Official Airline Guide, Official Hotel and Resort Guide,** and **World Travel Directory.** They are extremely expensive volumes used in the travel industry. You can find them in the travel section of most major libraries.

Airlines

- Call various airlines and ask for any free brochures or pamphlets they may have that cover different destinations on your trip.

National tourist offices

- For good general background information and some helpful tips, write to the national tourist office of each country you think you want to visit. You can ask for hotel and restaurant guides; sightseeing information; lists of gardens, castles, museums, spas; travel maps; and so on.

- Note that tourist offices shy away from questions of comparison (Is one hotel better than another? Should we go here instead of there?). The more specific your question, the more difficult it may be for a country's tourist office to answer. Use toll-free numbers from your phone book to call airlines serving the countries you're interested in for addresses and phone number. Write to the office nearest your home, or your letter may be returned.

- Write to them well ahead of your planned departure date, and allow as much time as possible for a reply.

AGENTS AND AGENCIES

In the past, the traveler who walked into a travel agency could safely be assumed to be innocent—and rich. **Good** agents can find super bargains amidst the garble of airlines and tour brochures. Still, it's really a customer's responsibility to do reading and research before going to a travel agent. This will make your relationship more professional!

- You will probably save money planning and arranging for your trip by yourself if you're a free spirit, if you're aggressive and resourceful, and if you're ready to study up on alternatives in transportation, food, and lodging.

- Even if you fit that description, an agent may know of tour packages that are so cheap that you can still save money while using only some of their features. So don't rule out travel agencies without checking to see what they have to offer.

- If you don't want to plan and arrange for your trip yourself, a well-chosen agent can be a fine resource. Don't walk in and say to him, "I want to go to these twelve cities. Book me flights and rooms." If you do, you'll pay through the nose! Instead, ask for tours to match your interests and then have the agent alter them if necessary.

- In short, shop around. Compare what an agent can do with what you can do, balance the benefits and costs, and act accordingly.

Picking an agency

- Larger agencies tend to have more clout than smaller ones. It may be more personal and more convenient to go to a neighborhood agent, but what happens if something goes wrong abroad? Find out whether or not the agency has a 24-hour emergency service, just in case something does go wrong.

- Ask the agency what kind of travel it specializes in. If it doesn't match your travel plans, ask the agency to refer you to another agency specializing in your brand of travel.

- In special cases, you may want to work with agents in other cities. If the best agency for skiing tours happens to be in New York, carry on your business through the mail.

Recognizing a good agent

Good travel agents are harder to find than the American Society of Travel Agents would like to admit. Unfortunately, many of them are in the business more for low-cost travel for themselves than for their clients.

On the other hand, some agents are outstanding. Most of the good ones specialize in some way: low-cost tours, luxury travel, study groups, ski vacations, incentive travel, business, etc.

- Most travel agents are members of the American Society of Travel Agents (ASTA), so be wary of those who are not. ASTA maintains a file of complaints. You can write or call them at 711 Fifth Avenue, New York, NY 10022: (212) 486-0700.

- Look for the intials CTC—for Certified Travel Consultant—after an agent's name. This designation signifies that he is a person of good reputation who has been through a specialized course.

- Find out whether someone in the agency is familiar with the specific area you plan to visit. If you find such a person, you can learn a great deal—and in addition he will be able to reserve flights, make reservations, and book you into tours as part of his general travel assistance to you.

WHEN TO GO

A great deal of fiction has been written about the wonderful weather in Europe. Don't be conned by this propaganda, which is more wishful thinking than fact. The bikini-clad women in the pictures in travel brochures were photographed in the August heat, not in the dead of winter, as promoters would have you believe. The guidelines below cover the best times to visit various parts of Europe. The Climate Chart in the Appendix has more details.

Travel seasons

- Travel to **Scandinavia** during the summer, which lasts from mid-May to early October. Not only is the weather good during this period, but you will also be able to take advantage of the long days. Just the opposite is true during the winter, which is snowy and dark—so dark that "sightseeing" becomes a joke.

- Visit **central Europe** (including the British Isles and Germany) from late April to late October, if one of your main concerns is good weather. Much of this area experiences heavy rainfall, so bring a good umbrella and the best raincoat you can afford. You'll find some of Europe's most fascinating cities in this belt, however—and if you see them during the off season, you can take advantage of smaller crowds and lower prices.

- Winters in **southern Europe** are not as mild as some people would like you to believe. True, you'll run into sunny winter days. But don't expect to brave the chill of Mediterranean or Atlantic waters. Furthermore, summers can get so hot in the south that you will rather do what the natives do from noon until late afternoon—sleep in a cool place. Unless, of course, you're lucky enough to be on a beach by the sea—the other obvious alternative, one chosen by Greeks, Italians, French, and Portuguese, young and old.

- Some places do offer good to excellent off-season weather. In the fair to good category: the **Balearics** (Majorca, Menorca, and Ibiza) and **Madeira.** Just a little better: **Sicily.** Better yet: **Rhodes.** And the most reliable for warm winter sun: the **Canaries.**

HOW LONG TO STAY

The length of your trip may be predetermined by the time you have available for your vacation, so that you feel you have little leeway in this regard. However, if it's at all possible, try to make a trip to Europe last at least three weeks. This will give you the time to enjoy and savor the European scene.

- Subtract three days from the overall length of your trip. The first, and probably the last, day of any trip will be wasted, and you may have to spend the second day recuperating somewhat from your transatlantic flight.

- Write off at least part of any day spent traveling long distances, as from one city to the next.

- Fight the urge to see all of Europe in ten days, and arrange to spend more time in fewer places. If you slow down, your trip will be more enjoyable.

The following simple chart indicates the minimum recommended lengths of stay in European countries. Periods are given in days, and do not include the time needed for transportation into and out of the country.

Minimum Recommended Stays in European Countries

Andorra . . . . . . One day	**Ireland** . . . . Three days
Austria . . . . Five days, with three days in Vienna	**Italy** . . . . Ten days, with four days in Rome, three in Florence, one in Venice
Azores . . . . Three days	
Belgium . . . . . . Three days, with two days in major cities	**Liechtenstein** . Half a day
	Luxembourg . . One day
Canaries . . . . . Three days	**Madeira** . . . . . . Two days
Corsica . . . . . . Two days	**Majorca** . . . . . . Two days
Crete . . . . Two days	**Malta** . . . . One day
Denmark . . . . . Three days, with two days in Copenhagen	**Netherlands** . . Three days, with two days in Amsterdam
Finland . . . . . . Two days	**Norway** . . . . . . Three days
France . . . . Ten days, with five days in Paris	**Portugal** . . . . . . Five days, with two days in Lisbon
Germany . . . . . Four days, with two days in Munich	**Sardinia** . . . . . . One day
	Sicily . . . . One day
Gibraltar . . . . . One day	**Spain** . . . . Ten days, with three days in Madrid and Toledo combined
Great Britain . . Ten days, with five days in London	
Greece . . . . Seven days, with three days on mainland	**Sweden** . . . . . . One day
	Switzerland . . . Four days
Iceland . . . . One day	**Yugoslavia** . . . . Three days

HOW FAR AND HOW FAST

If this is your first trip to Europe, you may be inclined to travel fast and far, to give yourself a sneak preview of trips to come. It is totally natural to want to do this, and high-speed travel can be exhilarating. The trouble is, it's also exhausting and costs a bundle.

You will find that the more you try to see, the less you will really see. That's what could be called the "today-is-Tuesday-this-must-be-Brussels" syndrome. Many tours operate on this kind of plan, giving you a smattering of many cities rather than a deeper profile of several.

Planning trip mileage

* To help you enjoy your trip more fully, use the mileage chart and a map to plan your itinerary. Decide which cities you'd like to see. You might trace your route in red with a felt-tipped pen. Now add up the mileage to see just how far you plan to go.

* Divide the total mileage by the number of days you'll be in Europe. (Don't count the first and last days.)

* If you are traveling by train or car, don't plan to cover more than 150 miles per day. The same rule applies to traveling on a tour bus. Naturally, you will sometimes wind up having traveled farther than this average distance. If you consistently cover much more than 150 miles per day, however, your trip will turn out to have been too expensive and time-consuming, as well as too tiring.

* If you will be flying between two points, ignore the mileage between them—and simply write off one full day. Do this for each plane trip you'll be taking. Subtract these days from the total number of days you'll be abroad (minus the first and last days). This will give you a good idea of how many days you'll have left to enjoy Europe.

* If you find that you'll be traveling too far in too short a time, admit it. Here are some options: cut down on the number of cities to be seen, extend your trip to make your travel time more enjoyable, or plan a second trip for a later date. With the possible exception of Venice, most European cities will still be there in years to come.

Structuring short trips

The shorter the trip, the more organized it must be! If you have very little time, you won't want to spend any of it waiting in reservation lines. Every phase of the trip should be planned to help you avoid waits. You should have all reservations for plane flights, all reservations for hotel rooms, and reservations for fancier restaurants made well in advance of arrival. If you plan to attend the theater, festivals, musical events, the opera, or any popular tourist attractions requiring tickets, you should have all tickets in hand (when possible) or reservations confirmed in writing (when not).

- Don't leave anything to chance.
- Limit yourself to one carry-on bag to cut baggage claim time.
- Note that you'll pay extra for a structured trip, but it will be worth every penny.

Structuring long trips

If you've got three weeks or more to play around with, you might want to follow a much looser program. Some people get by without any rservations at all, allowing themselves extra time to find a room, obtain tickets to the theater, and so on. Their attitude is relaxed and easy-going, a sign that they are more experienced travelers.

- Note that the big advantage of this style of travel is that you have a choice: you're never bound by a prearranged schedule, you can shift travel plans daily, you can move out of a hotel you don't like, you can seek out intimate restaurants on your own—in short, you can do just about anything at whim.

- Loosely structured travel appeals greatly to younger travelers with lots of time to spend. But it's gaining popularity with older people as well, because it has another great advantage over structured travel: it's less expensive. When you get into the European section of this guide, you'll discover how easy it is to cut costs if you begin to "think European."

Mileage Between European Cities

	Amsterdam	Barcelona	Berlin	Bordeaux	Brussels	Calais	Copenhagen	Dublin	Florence	Geneva	Hamburg	Helsinki	Lisbon	London	Madrid	Marseilles	Milan	Munich	Naples	Nice	Oslo	Paris	Rome	Stockholm	Venice
Barcelona	950																								
Berlin	450	1215																							
Bordeaux	660	405	1015																						
Brussels	125	810	490	535																					
Calais	235	800	620	555	130																				
Copenhagen	590	1355	465	1185	655	780																			
Dublin	565	965	950	830	460	330	1115																		
Florence	775	730	810	815	995	880	1215	1215																	
Geneva	545	490	690	440	415	470	985	800	495																
Hamburg	290	1135	185	905	370	505	215	785	970	705															
Helsinki	1025	1865	970	1685	1185	1285	500	1615	1715	1485	720														
Lisbon	1365	785	1690	755	1245	1260	1895	1595	1455	1190	1690	2395													
London	305	725	690	570	200	70	855	260	935	540	525	1355	1335												
Madrid	1145	385	1445	440	965	945	1815	1275	1110	680	1335	2115	400	1015											
Marseilles	800	355	965	415	675	690	1235	1000	415	265	970	1735	1190	740	705										
Milan	670	650	700	740	635	620	1060	950	200	230	770	1560	1430	690	1050	355									
Munich	535	830	375	755	495	510	775	900	440	320	480	1275	1675	640	1415	610	310								
Naples	1160	1055	1135	1110	1320	1145	1540	1475	325	795	1190	2040	1145	1215	1435	730	515	765							
Nice	815	420	920	515	690	790	1255	1010	295	300	1090	1785	805	750	805	120	220	535	595						
Oslo	865	1645	805	1565	1030	1160	380	1490	1590	1370	510	445	2240	1230	1995	1615	1440	1155	1920	1660					
Paris	315	685	690	350	185	210	835	505	745	325	550	1335	1105	245	780	480	560	495	1060	580	1215				
Rome	955	915	995	970	1030	1180	1400	1335	185	650	1060	1900	1700	1075	1295	590	390	625	130	465	1780	930			
Stockholm	920	1760	865	1580	1080	1005	395	1510	1610	1380	615	105	2290	1250	2010	1630	1455	1170	1935	1680	340	1230	1795		
Venice	740	825	700	930	875	790	1105	1125	170	405	815	1115	1650	865	960	550	175	325	460	370	995	690	355	1010	
Vienna	820	1155	625	1055	750	890	1030	1175	550	645	565	1305	1945	915	1700	930	505	255	955	730	1180	815	820	1200	380

Calais to Nice = 790÷3 = 263 per day.
– Paris = 210.

3

TRAVEL PARTNERS AND TOURS

Should you make a trip by yourself, with a friend or spouse, with a group of people you like, or as part of a tour group? Should you take the kids or a baby? There's no easy answer, although the answer's often taken for granted—especially in the case of couples. The hints in this chapter should be helpful to you, not only in making your decision, but also in living with it!

SOLO TRAVEL

There are many advantages to traveling alone: you can do as you damn well please, when you damn well please, at your own pace, with or without someone else along, as you choose. In short, you have total freedom.

On the other hand, you pay for such freedom. If you go on a tour, you may be socked with a surcharge. If you're totally on your own, you will have no way of sharing bills at mealtime, in the hotel, and for personal transportation. It's all out of your pocket and only your pocket.

You may also be lonely—but loneliness can be converted into an advantage, as it will force you to get to know Europeans and other travelers.

Traveling alone and liking it

- As a loner, take advantage of short and inexpensive tours to popular tourist sights. You'll not only meet people, but also keep your costs down.

- Be willing to share the cost of a room. If you are concerned about sharing a room with a stranger, put anything of value in the hotel safe.

- When faced with the prospect of eating alone, bring a newspaper, a book, or writing paper with you to the restaurant. If you meet someone interesting, fine; if not, you will catch up on your reading.

- Go a little before or after the peak dinner hour, to avoid running into poor treatment at the hands of waiters, as solo travelers sometimes do.

- A travel agency that caters to solo travelers: Gramercy Singleworld Travel, 444 Madison Ave., New York, NY 10022, 800-223-6490 or (212) 753-7595.

- Resort villages that cater mainly to solo travelers (although families and couples are now welcome): Club Med, 40 West 57th Street, New York, NY 10019, 800-528-3100 or (212) 977-2100.

Women traveling alone

Most solo travel takes place without a hitch, even for women traveling alone. Just a little common sense added to the spirit of adventure will get you by—almost anywhere!

- Travel light. Read the section on packing (p. 67) very carefully. Remember that the weight of your luggage will affect both your attitude and your vulnerability.

- Try to get by with a single piece of luggage. If you have to carry your own bags into a hotel lobby, everyone will immediately know that you're alone. If you can manage with a piece of luggage no larger than a big purse or briefcase-size bag, no one will have any way of knowing you're by yourself.

- Do not hitchhike. Although many women encounter few, if any, problems hitchhiking in Europe, the police files are filled with exceptions to prove the rule: hitchhiking is more dangerous for women than for men, especially for women traveling alone.

- Make use of inexpensive public transportation instead of hitchhiking. Second-class train travel won't break the bank and can be combined with travel on buses, trams, subways, and trolleys to get you just about anywhere. You'll meet many fascinating people traveling on public transportation—the low-risk, low-cost way to travel.

- When using any form of private transportation, never travel alone—and this includes taxis. Robbery—and rape—in taxis are common enough to be frightening.

- If you're attacked, scream and shout.

- Womantour, 5314 North Figueroa Street, Los Angeles, CA 90042, organizes both group and individual tours for women alone.

Special considerations for women

You should know that women in southern European countries do not go out alone at night—with the exception of prostitutes. And with the exception of foreign women who don't know better. Even if you're with another woman, you can still be hassled.

It's best to find an escort for evening entertainment or to rely on taxis to get you to and from restaurants, night clubs, and hotels. Even cab drivers will hassle a woman traveling alone at night.

If you travel alone in Italy and Spain, you must cope with the aggressive behavior of men. In these countries, men will pinch women's fannies—extremely hard. This sounds funny to everyone except to the woman who finds herself black and blue. Three suggestions:

- Have someone you trust walk directly behind you in a crowd. And place your back against a wall when riding in an elevator.

- Walk against, not with, the main flow of pedestrian traffic when you can.

- If you know who's doing the pinching (it can be hard as hell to figure out!), turn and face him. Say "**Basta!**" in a firm, no-nonsense tone of voice. This means "Enough!" —and that's usually enough.

TWOSOME AND FAMILY TRAVEL

The big advantages of staying together are shared company and shared costs. A room for a couple may only be a few dollars more than it would be for a solo traveler. In many instances, the same savings apply to food and transportation. In short, it costs far less for two people to travel together than to go independently. But savings mean nothing unless you're both doing what you really want to do.

Traveling as a twosome

- If you and your partner cannot agree on the purpose of a trip, consider traveling independently. You may prefer completely different destinations, so why not go your separate ways?

- Meet again in places you'd both like to visit.

- Carry your own bags, unless you're willing to pay someone else to do it for you. It is unfair to ask a partner to carry luggage.

- Share all responsibilities with your partner. Anyone who has to make most of the decisions shoulders the burden for any mistakes made. That burden should be equally divided.

- Iron out all money matters before you start. Good reckoning makes good friends.

Family travel

The more people involved in a European trip, the more complex the planning is going to be. You can't expect to suit all tastes at all times when working with a group.

- Make sure that each person in the family has a say in planning the trip.
- Gear the pace of the trip to that of the youngest member of the group.
- Agree that all responsibilities shall be shared.
- Since each person will carry his own luggage, make sure that the size of the bag matches the size of the person.
- If children are along, allow time for numerous breaks in the itinerary: for a trip to the beach, a hike through the woods, a pause for an ice cream cone.
- Note that younger children can appreciate cathedrals, churches, and art galleries—in small doses. Children tend to be activity-oriented, which means that they'd rather go to a beach than to the cathedral at Chartres —or would rather combine the two, preferably in a period of twenty minutes!
- Allow for the option of splitting up the party from time to time, so that those primarily interested in cultural attractions can have adequate time to appreciate them.
- Remember that families of all nationalities congregate in campgrounds, which makes them very enjoyable for most children.

Traveling with a baby

- When making reservations for air travel, try to schedule departure and arrival times so that they do not coincide with the baby's feedings. Avoid the peak or rush hours as well, choosing a less popular flight time.
- Contact the airline well in advance if you wish to reserve a bassinet. Ask about pre-boarding privileges.
- Bring milk if you're feeding the baby from a bottle. Ask a stewardess to warm it up when she's not busy serving drinks or meals.
- Be sure to have something for the baby to drink during takeoff and landing: the sucking will relieve the pressure that builds up in the baby's ears.
- Bring a towel to cover you during feeding and to place under the baby at changing time.

- Bring a small blanket, plastic bags for disposable diapers, small toys for the baby to play with, and a folding (umbrella) stroller. The stroller will make it much easier for you both to get around, and you can lift it into a booth in a restaurant without waking the baby up.

- Since many European restaurants welcome children at noon, but look coldly upon them in the evening, plan larger meals in the middle of the day and snacks at night.

- Note that babysitters are available at many European hotels, but that they are quite expensive.

- Note: if you are traveling by car, you must buy or bring some sort of safety harness that will fit into the back seat, as it is against the law in most European countries for small children to ride in the front seat of a car.

TOURS

Tours can be the answers to travelers' prayers or forms of temporary damnation. The most important question for you to ask yourself, then, is whether you are a good prospect for a tour. Loners should not take tours. Most people who are impatient standing in lines will not like tours. Impulsive, free-spirited people often regret traveling on tours.

On the other hand, people who dislike unplanned weekends, who are not very aggressive, who lead scheduled lives, and who don't speak foreign languages find tours an excellent way to travel. For those in poor health, joining a tour may be more attractive than traveling alone. In short, it's a question of personality. If you do decide to join a tour, be sure its goals and your own goals are similar.

Advantages of tours

- Tours can save you money. You're joining a group that buys everything as a block, which ensures substantial price reductions across the board.

- Tours can be prepaid, allowing you to know in advance how much the trip is going to cost. You can also put off payment by financing the trip.

- Tour packages, which cover all your major expenses, allow you to pay in dollars. In this way you avoid the currency exchange rip-off.

- Tours can be located that are tailored to individual needs or interests, from skiing to bird-watching.

- Tours offer companionship for travelers prone to loneliness.

- Tours help less aggressive travelers cope with the language barrier and avoid embarrassing situations.

- Tours have clout, the ability to get you into a hotel or restaurant in peak tourist seasons.

- Tours save you time and energy by preventing potential hassles.

- Tours are organized by experts who know the most interesting sights to see. They generally hire competent travel guides in each city to help you understand its beauty, history, and tradition.

Disadvantages of tours

- Tours herd people together. To find out how you react to this experience, go to a local museum or industrial plant and take a tour with a group of people there. If it's enjoyable, you may also enjoy taking a tour abroad. If you find out that this just isn't for you, avoid foreign tours!

- Tours can be hurried, impersonal, and flavorless affairs. Throughout the trip you will be bound to follow a prearranged schedule, oriented to a group and its needs. It may take the travail out of travel, but it can also wring the lust out of wanderlust.

- The normal mode of transportation for tour groups in Europe is the bus. It's convenient and usually comfortable, but it can be equally boring and confining.

- You pay for a tour sight unseen, which is something like marrying the same way. There's no real chance for a refund if things go awry.

- Tours are groups of people, people whom you may or may not like. But they'll be your companions anyway.

- The words in tour brochures are just that—words. A "first-class" hotel may end up being, well, second-rate, even in Soho!

- Most tour contracts squirm with loopholes and catches

- Tours isolate you from contact with local people by taking care of everything for you.

- If you don't like the hotels chosen for you or the restaurants' bland fare, your complaints may fall on deaf ears.

- In some cases, you could do much better from a financial standpoint by not taking a tour. The luxury tours are a good example—Jason could have picked up a bucketful of golden fleece sheared from wealthy tourgoers!

Tour Package Checklist

If you take the trouble to consult tour brochures or agents and find answers to the following questions, you will be in a much better position to judge the quality of any tour package you're considering.

- ☐ Is the tour operator a member of the United States Tour Operators' Association? (Most of these operators are reliable.)
- ☐ How much will the tour cost altogether?
- ☐ Will a service charge be added on? If so, how much will it be? Often you'll find that there is a service charge outlined in very fine print at the end of the brochure. Words like "extra," "optional" and "bonus" should also be red flags to you.
- ☐ What extra or supplemental charges will apply to you? What will optional packages cost you? How much is the advance deposit?
- ☐ What are the penalties for cancellation?
- ☐ Are substitutions allowed on the passenger list?
- ☐ Can the dates of the tour be changed arbitrarily?
- ☐ Can the schedule or itinerary be rearranged for any reason?
- ☐ Can the tour be cancelled? How much notice must be given?
- ☐ Does the tour include transportation to and from the airport? Most tours don't.
- ☐ Does the tour cost include the full price of airfare to and from Europe? What are the dates and times of flights? Are the flights nonstop?
- ☐ Does the tour price cover all airport departure taxes?
- ☐ What kind of transportation is provided for in Europe?
- ☐ Does it include all transfers from airports and train stations? Does it include the cost of transportation to meals and night life?
- ☐ What kind of intercity transportation is provided: bus, train, air?
- ☐ If it's a bus, is it air conditioned, or "air cooled" (a tour brochure expression meaning that the windows can be opened)?
- ☐ If it's a plane or a train, what class will you be in?
- ☐ How many nights' accommodation is included in the tour price? Are there any nights where the cost of a room has been left out?
- ☐ Is there a supplemental charge if you want a room to yourself? How much?
- ☐ Which hotels will you be staying in? Get the names.
- ☐ Can other hotels be substituted arbitrarily? If so, get the names.
- ☐ What's included in the room? Bath or shower? Two beds? Get details.
- ☐ Where are the hotels located? Tell them to show you on a map.
- ☐ Are all tips and taxes included in the room price?
- ☐ Is there any charge whatsoever that's not included?
- ☐ Are all meals included in the price of the tour? Is any meal not included? If not, why not? Or if not, where not?
- ☐ Where will you be eating? In the hotel? In a restaurant? What restaurants?
- ☐ What's included with the meal? Is wine included? Is coffee included? Is dessert included? Is anything excluded? If so, how much will it cost?
- ☐ Do you have a choice from the menu at each meal? Can you make substitutions at no extra charge?
- ☐ Are all tips and service charges for meals included in the tour price?
- ☐ Who pays the entrance fee to museums, galleries, and events?
- ☐ What is the pace of the tour? Does it leave you any free time?
- ☐ Does the tour spend enough time in each city to let you get anything out of the visit?
- ☐ Will the tour have an escort? Will the same escort be with the tour for the whole time (valuable)?
- ☐ Will the tour have travel guides for each city?
- ☐ Does the tour include insurance for accidents, health, baggage, etc.? If so, how much? Any deductible? Any exclusions?
- ☐ Who takes care of the baggage? Is there any extra cost? Are all tips to porters included in the cost of the hotel room?

4
TRANSPORTATION TO EUROPE

BY PLANE

Almost everyone flies to Europe today, because air travel is faster and cheaper than ocean travel. Yet, on every flight, some passengers wind up paying as much as three or four times what some others pay. Smart travelers know this and learn strategies to keep costs down.

General money-saving strategies

- Buy all your tickets for transatlantic travel in the United States. If you buy tickets abroad, you'll have to pay for them in foreign currency at a preset rate of exchange, which may cost you extra money.

- Be sure to ask the airline or travel agent for full information on stopover and extension privileges. Most transatlantic tickets can include inter-European flights as well. Note that special excursion fares can be reserved in the United States, but must be paid for abroad. Travel agents neither promote nor encourage the sale of these tickets because they do not make a commission on them, but ask about them anyway.

- All students should contact CIEE (see p. 16) for information on inter-European plane travel. It can save you 40 to 75 percent of regular fares.

- Flights to and from minor cities within a foreign country may be no more expensive than flights to major ones. You may save yourself the price of a train or plane fare to a small town by asking whether your fare would take you there in the first place—at no extra charge!

- When paying for tickets on a nondiscounted basis, such as regular coach or first class, be sure to have the airline or travel agent explain all the advantages, including bonus mileage, which may allow you to stop off at a number of different destinations that you may never have thought of visiting on your own.

Comparison shopping

- Spend some time on the phone getting different quotes on comparable flights on various airlines. Since the market has opened up competitively, prices do vary along identical routes.

- Watch for introductory fares or special coupon offers. As airlines open up new routes, they offer incentives to new customers in the form of reduced fares. These tend to be heavily advertised in local newspapers—so stay alert to the possibility of coming up with a once-in-a-lifetime bargain!

- Use the toll-free or 800 numbers (listed in your phone book) when you call the airlines.

Asking the right question

- Let the person on the other end of the phone know immediately that you're bargain-hunting by asking for the lowest fare from A to B.

- Ask whether there are any incentive fares.

- Find out whether there are reductions for midweek flights.

- Ask whether you can save money by flying to a less popular city near your final destination.

- Even after you've arranged for a flight, continue to watch for better deals. If a bargain pops up, turn in your ticket and go with the better fare. In some cases, you'll save money even if you must pay a penalty for canceling!

- If you buy a ticket with a credit card and then have to cancel or change your travel plans, ask for a **refund receipt** when you return the ticket for credit. Note the ticket number, and the date and place you bought it, so that you can contact the credit card company if the credit does not show up on your bill.

Comparing prices

Once you've come up with the lowest price possible by comparison shopping among the larger airlines, compare the fare with those offered by Icelandair (Icelandic) and Laker. These maverick airlines provide an accurate barometer of prevailing low fares.

- **Icelandair** should be listed in your phone book. It has a branch in the south listed under International Air Bahamas. If you fly Icelandair, you'll stop off in Iceland and continue on to Luxembourg City. The inconvenience may be worth the extra savings. That's for you to

decide. Call the airlines for up-to-date flight information and prices.

- **Laker** operates a shuttle to Great Britain from Los
Angeles and New York. The airline now offers contin-
uous ticket sales, which it did not do in the past. If the
present day's flights are filled, you can reserve seats
for the following day, making a wait in line worthwhile.
Call (212) 995-2113 in New York or (213) 646-9600 or
646-9650 in Los Angeles for details on buying tickets
and current prices.

- If you drive to New York to take advantage of Laker's
shuttle, you can leave your car with Auto Baby Sitters,
827 Sterling Place, Brooklyn, NY 11216. Check with
them for their long-term rates.

Buying tickets in advance

- Since only a certain number of seats is allotted for
highly reduced fares on any given flight, you can save
hundreds of dollars by buying a ticket far in advance of
a planned trip. In short, the early bird does get the
worm.

- Note that the airline cannot raise the price once you've
paid for the ticket. (This does not apply in Europe,
however.)

Keeping flexible about travel dates

- Be as flexible as possible in your travel plans so that
you can take advantage of lower rates. What if you have
to leave on a Thursday instead of a Friday or return on a
Monday instead of a Sunday? Isn't it worth a hundred-
dollar bill?

- Be sure to ask about **excursion rates**, with minimum
and maximum lengths of stay in Europe. It may be that,
by adding or subtracting a few days from your planned
trip, you can save yourself a good deal of money.

- Ask the airline whether a **standby fare** exists on the
route you're planning to take. This will make sense in
the not-so-popular months from October to April.
Standby status is for the most flexible travelers, of
course.

Off-season travel

The weather may not be so hot in the off season (from Novem-
ber to March), but the savings are substantial.

- Note that you'll also find slightly lower fares in the
"shoulder seasons" of spring and fall. Contact the
airlines for exact cutoff dates for each season. Maybe

you can take advantage of lower rates by changing your trip dates by no more than a week or two.

Using travel agents

It costs no more to buy a ticket through a travel agent than to buy one directly from the airline. The problem is that many agents do not like working with discounted fares, because they make a commission on the total dollar value of tickets sold.

- Don't be afraid to comparison shop with travel agents. Make it clear with each one that you want to know the best deal to get you from A to B.

- Note: sometimes an agent will come up with a tour fare that will cost less than comparable airfare. I know this sounds impossible, but it isn't. If you decide to discard all land arrangements of the tour to tootle off on your own, that's fine. You will still have come up with a bargain.

- Never assume that agents are infallible. Check and recheck all tickets purchased through them for possible errors.

Trouble-savers for booking reservations

- Call before 7:00 a.m. or after 7:00 p.m. to get through to the airline without a long wait.

- Make a point of being very specific. Repeat the day and date several times to avoid mixups. Get the name of the person helping you. Mark down the date and time of your call along with the information concerning your flight.

- Try to book nonstop or at least direct flights, so that you won't have to get off the plane.

- If you do have to make connections, try to fly with the same airline, so as to avoid long walks and check-in hassles at the connecting airport. Airlines usually have a block of gates in each terminal; if you fly with one airline, you'll have only a short walk to a connecting flight.

- Note: airline tickets can be purchased on credit, with charges varying with repayment schedule. Compare these with rates available from your bank to come up with the best loan terms.

Picking up tickets

- Pay for and pick up tickets in advance, so as to avoid the crush at the airport. It's a good feeling to have the ticket in your pocket, an assurance that no one will now be able to bungle your important reservation.

- When you get your tickets, be sure to check the dates, flight times, and flight numbers on them for accuracy. Read all materials closely so you know your rights.

- If someone does bungle it, you've got the clerk's name; if nothing happens to resolve the problem, ask to speak to a supervisor. Be polite, calm, and firm. **Persistence will pay off** (and squeaky voices get oiled).

- Don't leave the return date blank, even if you are traveling without a set date of return. Have the clerk fill it in with an approximate date of return. For some reason, it is easier to make a new reservation when you have an already-dated, versus an open, ticket.

Seat selection

- Find out about available aircraft and best seats at the time you pick up your ticket—not later, in the hurried atmosphere of the departure lounge. Ask to see a seating chart, choose where you'd like to be (mark down some alternates), and reserve a seat right away if you can. If you can't do so, mark down the seat choices on your ticket folder so that you can ask for them when checking in at the gate (see p. 83 for tips on choosing seats).

BY SHIP

Going to Europe by ship is the old-style, romantic way of getting there. In good weather it's a vacation in itself. Not only can the food and company be great, but such a trip also allows for a gradual adaptation to time changes. If you've got lots of time and enough money, going by ship is highly recommended.

But note the disadvantages: ocean travel is very expensive for most people, costing far more than airfare. It takes time—from five to ten days, depending upon the size of the ship. In rough weather, most people do get sick; even if you do not, you'll be stuck on board with everyone else.

General strategies for cruises

- When choosing a cabin, position yourself as far as possible from noise and vibration. The lower you go in a ship, the nearer you are to the engines and generators. Pay the higher fare to get a quiet room on an upper deck.

- Start taking seasickness pills a day or two before you leave. Otherwise they won't do the job.

- Bring a bottle of your favorite booze. You can purchase

alcohol on board by the bottle, but it's only delivered on the day you debark. Bringing some aboard will cut high bar bills.

- Take advantage of free services: seconds at meals, extra wine, extra dessert, afternoon snacks and teas, late-night snacks, free movies, etc.

Tipping on board

- Ask about company policy on tipping before you buy a ticket. Tips may be included in the ticket price. If they are, the ticket is really costing you about fifty dollars less than a comparable ticket on a line where tips are not included.

- If tips are not included, tip room stewards, waiters, and other service staff. The more service you ask for, the more you should expect to tip. Tips are best given immediately for such services as bringing late-night snacks.

- One very effective way of tipping: hand the room steward or waiter an amount adding up to half the tip you expect to give him altogether. Tell him exactly what you expect. And tell him that you will give him the other half of the tip at the end of the trip. This is up-front bargaining for good service.

5

TRANSPORTATION IN EUROPE

Where are you going to go in Europe? How great will the total distance be? Are you on a tight budget or can you spend a little more? When are you going to go? How much energy do you have? Are you going to travel by yourself, as a twosome, or in a group?

Not until you have answered each of these questions should you decide whether travel by plane, train, car, motorcycle—or by hitchhiking—makes sense for you. Each way has its advantages and disadvantages.

BASIC CONSIDERATIONS

If you start with a few basic considerations, you will have an easier time choosing the best mode of travel for yourself.

Saving money

- If you're traveling alone, you'll have to travel by train, by motorcycle, or by thumb if you want to save money.

- If you're traveling with one or more people, you can bring the cost of car travel down to ten cents a mile or less per person.

- If you're planning on plane travel for getting around Europe, you'll have to increase your budget, no matter how many are in your party.

Saving time

- Car travel is fine for short trips (less than 150 miles per day), but not for longer ones. It is just too time-consuming in most European countries.

- Train travel is superb for intercity trips of 300 miles or less. In fact, for short runs, a train will get you there as fast as a plane will.

- Planes are great for trips of 300 miles or longer.

- Hitchhiking is out.

Saving human energy

- Plane travel is superb, especially for long trips. (So is

going by tour bus.) Train travel is also great—if you've got a seat, if the trip lasts no more than eight hours, and if you have little luggage.

- Motoring and hitching are out. Driving in Europe re-quires an enormous amount of energy.

Getting off the beaten path

- Car travel (or hitching) is often the only way to do it. A car offers complete mobility and freedom, and a car is an absolute necessity in Greece and Yugoslavia.

- Train travel is OK, but not great. Trains will get you to most smaller towns, but only after interminable waits and enough transfers to puzzle an electrical engineer.

- Planes? You guessed it. They're useless!

Cost Per Mile of Various Modes of Transportation	
Mode of transportation	**Cost per mile**
Plane	An average of twenty-eight cents per plane mile per person.
Train	A first-class average of fifteen cents per train mile per person.
	A second-class average of ten cents per train mile per person.
Car	If you travel over 1,000 miles per week, it will cost **under** thirty-two cents per car mile.
	If you travel under 1,000 miles per week, it will cost you **over** thirty-two cents per mile.
	To find cost per person, divide cost per mile by number of people in car.
Motorcycle	An average of four cents per mile, not including initial pur-chase price.
Hitchhiking	No charge, unless you agree to split gas costs.

PLANES

If you want to travel widely in Europe in a relatively short time and are willing to pay the high cost, go ahead and take a plane.

Advantages of plane travel

- For city-to-city trips of 300 miles or more, plane travel is the fastest way.

- It's the only way to get to some places, including many of the more popular islands.

- For a solo traveler covering great distances, it can be the most economical way to see Europe.

- You waste little precious time getting from one place to another.

- It's safe—popular misconceptions aside.

Disadvantages of plane travel

- Plane travel can be expensive, especially for shorter city-to-city trips. It's doubly expensive for twosomes and exorbitant for groups.

- Plane trips are oriented to travel between major cities.

- Plane travel can actually be slower than train travel for trips of 200 miles and less.

- You've got to spend money and time on transfers.

- You can be locked in by bad weather.

- You pass over, not through the countryside.

Plane travel strategies

- Get all details about your plane travel worked out in the U.S. whenever possible. This includes your itinerary, confirmed reservations, and tickets for most flights.

- Have flights and flight times written on the ticket folder. It's also better to reserve a return seat on a tentative basis than to leave the return date open. If you have to change a reservation, just call it in.

- Check into stopover privileges whenever you buy a transatlantic ticket. Maybe you'll be able to see several cities en route to another one.

- Check into the possibility of adding another leg on to a ticket you've already purchased. It might be less expensive than buying a separate ticket.

- Get the free brochure from TWA that gives you the seating arrangements on some of the most popular aircraft.

- Contact TWA and other airlines for information about the special clubs and waiting rooms available in many airports, including a few in Europe. For a yearly fee, you can take advantage of them. These clubs are most useful for businesspeople and others who travel frequently.

Plane Fare Map

Use this map to figure out the approximate economy air fare for your entire trip. Note that fares change rapidly; this map is only meant to give you comparative costs.

Inter-European flights

- Note: London is one of the best bases for buying inexpensive tickets to many parts of Europe, Africa, and the Middle East. Of course, you'll have to spend time finding the bargains, but they're definitely there!

- Otherwise, try to buy all tickets for inter-European air travel in the U.S. You'll save money. For some flights, you'll find that you can reserve seats in the U.S., but will still have to pay for them abroad. You can try asking travel agents for help or information on this point, but you may find that some are ignorant of European excursion fares and some are unwilling to help because they don't make a commission on such sales.

TRAINS

Train travel is a sensible way to see Europe, especially if you're going from one major city to the next. It's also a low-cost, low-risk mode of transportation—but it has a few drawbacks, too.

Advantages of train travel

- You spend less money when you go by train. It is far cheaper than plane or car travel, especially for solo travelers.

- Train travel is not only safe, but also convenient, because it takes you from city center to city center with no transfers to pay and no weather delays.

- Train travel is less tiring than car travel.

- Going by train is the fastest way to cover short distances between major European cities, faster even than plane travel for trips of 150 to 300 miles.

- Best of all, you see the land: it can be a visual feast.

Disadvantages of train travel

- Each day on a train is wasted—unless trains turn you on.

- Since train travel is oriented to city centers, you may find it confining.

- Trains don't wait for you; you wait for them.

- Over an extended period of time, train travel becomes monotonous.

- Trains are crowded. The low price draws crowds like a bargain basement sale; the corridors are so full of so many people and packs that a trip to the WC becomes one long stutter of "please" and "I'm sorry."

Train Fare Map

Use this map to figure the approximate cost of train travel in first class. If you plan to travel second class, deduct one-third of the total cost. Note that fares change rapidly; this map is only meant to give you comparative costs.

Railway passes

There are four special European railway passes: the Eurailpass and Youthrailpass for continental Europe, the BritRailpass for Great Britain, and a pass for Ireland. The first three must be bought in the U.S. from American travel agents, whose commission is included in the price you pay. The pass for Ireland can be bought there. (Consult an agent for details on the BritRailpass and the Irish pass.)

Advantages of Eurailpasses

The Eurailpass offers you unlimited train travel in the following countries: Austria, Belgium, Denmark, Finland, France, Germany, Greece, Italy, Luxembourg, Netherlands, Norway, Portugal, Spain, Sweden, and Switzerland. It covers various lengths of travel time.

- You go first class, which is very comfortable and clean in most areas.
- You know your overall travel costs from the start, since you must prepay them in the U.S.
- You never have to exchange currency for tickets.
- You can bypass boring ticket lines.
- You won't have to explain things to the conductor in foreign languages.
- You're free to plan your itinerary yourself.
- You can take almost any train in Europe without paying a surcharge.
- You won't have to pay to take the ferry from Brindisi in southern Italy to Greece, or the ferry from Stockholm to Finland.

Disadvantages of Eurailpasses

- Although you don't have to buy tickets, you do have to make reservations for the popular trains, including the TEEs (Trans Europe Express trains; see p. 50). That means some standing in lines.
- You have to pay $1.50 for each reservation.
- The pass is not honored on privately owned railroads, which may link up parts of your trip. Check ahead to avoid problems.
- If you lose your pass after it has been validated, you can never get a refund.

When to buy a Eurailpass

If you intend to travel fast and far, buy one. The longer-term passes are most economical, because they cut the cost per mile. Buy one if you intend to travel more than

- 1,900 miles in fifteen days,
- 2,300 miles in three weeks,
- 2,800 miles in one month,
- 3,900 miles in two months, or
- 4,600 miles in three months.

When not to buy a Eurailpass

- Don't buy one if you'll be visiting a few major cities that are close together. You'll do much better buying second-class tickets for those few runs.
- Consider buying a short-term pass and one or two other train tickets, to get the best of both worlds.

Youthrailpasses

The Youthrailpass, available to anyone under 26, is a variation of the Eurailpass offering two months of second-class rail travel for a set price of $260.

- The catch: you must specify the starting date of the pass's validity period before going abroad.

Doing without Eurailpasses

- Even if you don't buy a Eurailpass, you can save money by buying rail tickets in the U.S.
- You can save more by traveling second class. But go first class in Greece, Italy, Portugal, and Spain, where second class can be a zoo.

Getting train seats reserved

- Get seat reservations in the U.S. for the most popular trains, particularly the TEEs (see p. 157) whether you get a Eurailpass or not.
- Reservations can be made one month in advance for most trains; two months in advance for TEEs.
- Travel agents can make reservations for you. Since you'll pay for the reservation plus a cable fee of a dollar or two for each reservation, ask what the charge will be first.

CARS

Car travel is for independent spirits who are aware that freedom has its price. It's the best way to see Europe if you want to strike out to unusual and offbeat locations. Sightseeing, picnics, looking for charming hotels, checking out unusual restaurants, getting to out-of-the-way spots—all are open to motorists.

Advantages of car travel

- You don't have to worry about reservations, tickets, and ticket lines.
- You're free to change schedules at whim.
- You're part of the living jigsaw puzzle around you.
- You can go almost anywhere.
- It's economical for a group of three or more.
- It's comfortable, convenient, and fast.

Disadvantages of car travel

- If your trip is oriented to major cities, you will do better taking a train or plane.
- Car travel is expensive, far more expensive than most Americans realize.
- Purchase, rental, lease—all cost a great deal, making car travel prohibitive for solo travelers.
- Car travel is much slower than either train or plane travel. In most countries, it can take as much time to drive one mile as it would take to drive five to ten miles in the U.S.
- Car travel can insulate you from meeting Europeans.
- Finding a parking place in major European cities can be a migraine headache.

Buying, leasing, or renting a car

- Buying a car in Europe only makes sense if you plan to travel for three months or longer.
- Leasing can be a better option than rental for trips of five to ten weeks. Costs are still very high, so leasing will appeal mainly to three or four people traveling together.
- Renting has the greatest appeal to travelers on vacations lasting less than a month.

Comparison shopping for cars to buy abroad

Check around to come up with the best deal. If you do some comparison shopping, you'll shave off dollars on the initial cost of a foreign car!

- You can pick up many makes of foreign cars from Ship Side Showroom at Amsterdam Airport. For information, contact Ship Side Car Delivery, Inc., 609 Fifth Avenue, New York, NY 10017.

- Europe by Car, Inc., 45 Rockefeller Plaza, New York, NY 10020 will send you full information on buying a car abroad. Write them for information on current prices and models.

- Students can sometimes get a special discount on car purchase through the CIEE (see p. 16).

- You can also purchase cars for foreign delivery from local American dealers selling the brand of car you are interested in.

Car buying guide

- It's very important to check with U.S. Customs to make sure the car you're purchasing will pass pollution control standards, which may not be in force in Europe.

- If you intend to resell the car, ask the dealer about which models, options, and colors sell best. The best names for resale in the U.S. are BMW, Fiat, Mercedes-Benz, Porsche, Volkswagen, and Volvo.

- Plan ahead, especially for summer delivery. Order your car at least three months in advance.

- Find out the total cost, including all options, taxes, licenses, documents, and miscellaneous charges, and get it in writing. You will not have to pay major foreign taxes unless you keep the car for more than a year in the country where it was manufactured.

- Get the dealer's cost confirmed by the manufacturer, in writing.

- Make sure your agreement is for the newest model on the assembly line. If you're buying late in the year, order the next year's model. (Get the year down in writing, too!)

Car insurance

- Most American companies will not write policies covering European travel.

- Car manufacturers do write such policies, but at rip-off

prices. Be sure to ask the dealer to get you a brochure that outlines the rates before you sign any agreement.

- If the dealer has no idea of the rates, have him wire the manufacturer for them. Insist on knowing what they'll be ahead of time, so as to avoid hidden costs.

Car accessories

- Ask what the cost of a reflective triangle (Danger sign) and first-aid kit will be. European law requires all drivers to have these, and it's often much cheaper to bring your own from the U.S.

- Be attentive to details, such as the kind of tires to be put on the car. Paying for better ones now may be a good investment.

Taking delivery on a car

- Get the delivery date in writing, and have it confirmed in writing by the factory. When a car isn't delivered on that date, you have the right to ask the factory to pay for your room while you wait. They have the right to refuse, but they'll speed up delivery under pressure.

- Ask for delivery charges if you want to pick the car up somewhere else. There's no charge for delivery at the foreign plant.

- Plan to pay for the car with a certified check or traveler's checks. A sale can be completed in about an hour.

European warranties and service

European warranties and tissue paper have the same value. The former cover the car for from three to six months and include a series of so-called free service inspections, for which you get a coupon book. But only about half the service stations and garages that should honor the coupons will do so.

- Do some garage-hopping to find those that honor the coupons.

- Or be willing to pay for the "free" service for the sake of convenience.

Cars and camping

- To rent both cars and camping gear, contact Hendrik Hildebrandt, 61 Studiestraede, Copenhagen 1554, Denmark. Cars can be delivered to Amsterdam, Brussels, Frankfurt, Luxembourg, and Oslo for a forty-dollar charge. There is no charge for Copenhagen delivery.

Car leasing

This is really just long-term car rental with a discount, oriented to two or more people traveling together with the idea of splitting costs.

- Leasing is sensible for trips of a month or longer, but it is still very expensive. You can get information on leasing cars from the same outfits that rent them.

Car rental

- Get started early on your planning so that you can reserve a car well in advance of your arrival, especially if you will be abroad between May and September.

Base prices for car rental

The following chart shows how base prices vary by company for each country. If you choose a car from a company offering the best rate and can start your trip in a low-rate country, you'll save money.

Country	Cost/company			Country	Cost/company		
	A	B	C		A	B	C
Austria	200	199	208	Italy	221	198	194
Belgium	172	175	190	Luxembourg	166	257	204
Denmark	181	207	172	Netherlands	182	200	179
Finland	248	289	254	Norway	231	224	235
France	220	248	162	Portugal	129	123	126
Germany	182	182	201	Spain	134	166	103
Great Britain	159	145	123	Sweden	256	217	208
Greece	151	170	158	Switzerland	214	288	290
Ireland	99	164	126	Yugoslavia	166	184	198

Shopping around for rental rates

- Comparison shop before you rent. Using the toll-free (800) numbers in your telephone book, call major car rental firms such as Avis, Budget-Auto, Hertz, and National.

- Ask these companies to send you their free worldwide directories listing current car rental rates. You'll get fastest replies from Budget-Auto and Hertz (a few days' time). Avis takes about two weeks—and National, a month!

- Contact Europe by Car, Inc., 45 Rockefeller Plaza, New York, NY 10020, and ask for its rates. This firm also has offices in Chicago, Honolulu, Los Angeles, San Francisco, and Washington, DC.

- Note that airlines offer fly-and-drive tour packages, combining airfare and the cost of car rental in Europe. These are couple-oriented. You can get information on such packages from travel agents and airlines.
- Explore auto club discounts for members.
- Students should check with the CIEE (see p. 16) for rental discount information.
- Don't overlook foreign firms! During the off season, you can often find car rental bargains at foreign car rental firms, especially those in the suburbs of European cities.

Rental Taxes and Additional Fees

The base price is just that. You'll notice how the base price is augmented by taxes at the following rates:

Austria . . . . 18 percent tax plus a 1.2 percent contract fee
Belgium . . . . 16 percent tax (ask for information on 1.6 percent reduction)
Denmark . . . . 18 percent tax
Finland . . . . 16.28 percent tax
France . . . . 17.6 percent tax
Germany . . . . 12 percent tax
Great Britain . . . 8 percent tax
Greece . . . . 18 percent tax
Ireland . . . . 10 percent tax
Italy . . . . 14 percent tax plus 12 percent gas tax
Luxembourg . . . three-dollar tax (good deal)
Netherlands . . . . 18 percent tax (ask for the 1.8 percent reduction, saying that you'll be traveling outside the country)
Norway . . . . 20 percent tax
Portugal . . . . 4 percent tax
Spain . . . . 2.7 percent tax
Sweden . . . . taxes of 20.63 percent included in most base prices
Switzerland . . . . no tax
Yugoslavia . . . . . 15 percent tax plus a three-dollar tank-filling charge

If you plan to pick up your car in one city with the intention of leaving it off in another, you'll pay a fee in many instances. Ask about these charges when making a car rental reservation.

Rental pitfalls

- Do not plan on renting a car on any **island** where it's impossible to take out full insurance on the car. Avoid potential legal hassles by hiring a taxi on a daily basis instead.
- Never rent a car in **Great Britain** if you intend to cross the Channel with it. To avoid stiff surcharges and

premiums on insurance, leave the car in England and rent another car on the Continent!

- If you intend to travel extensively in **Italy**, rent your car outside the country. Only with foreign license plates can you take advantage of gasoline coupons (see p. 146).

MOTORCYCLES

You can go anywhere on a cycle—up rutted mountain paths or over to an old abandoned Moorish castle that's stranded miles from a main road. You're always close to the earth, the smell of mimosa trees or manure, the colors of bright red poppy fields or pastel-pink Portuguese walls, and the sounds of clicking tracks and buzzing mosquitoes or grape flies. It's an exciting sensation.

Advantages of motorcycle travel

- You can park a cycle almost anywhere.

- The gas costs are extremely low, since you'll get from sixty to ninety miles to the gallon.

- You can pass long lines of traffic anywhere, in the city or at borders.

- There's no doubt about it—it's an exciting way to travel!

Disadvantages of motorcycle travel

- The once-low initial cost of a bike is now very high.

- All mothers and lovers are afraid you'll fall. You will. But the odds are fifty-fifty that you'll survive the scraped knees, twisted feet, and close shaves.

- Bike-riding appears glamorous in the movies and on television. In real life, it can be dirty, tiring, cold, annoying, and frustrating. Have you ever changed a bike's tire and taken it off its rim by yourself? If not, you don't understand motorcycles, their absolute unreliability, the exhuastion of bike-riding, and the experiences you're in for.

- That's not all: you're at the mercy of the weather, a bike is easy to vandalize (you pay the high costs of garages), and a cycle is easy to steal.

- The rational conclusion would be never to buy a bike. Fortunately for motorcycle manufacturers, emotions run stronger than logic at times.

Buying a motorcycle abroad

- Buy a prestige bike for high resale value.

- Order the cycle for foreign delivery months in advance, since the supply may not cover the demand.

- Be willing to pick it up at the factory.

- Read the sections on buying and driving cars abroad (pp. 141-53) for other helpful hints.

- Remember that a cycle takes thousands of miles to break in (something you should point out when you sell it).

Motorcycle options

- Don't get a tank lock. When you're cold and exhausted, you don't want to have to undo your coat to look for a key. And tank locks rattle.

- Try to replace the side kickstand with any other kind. Side kickstands are useless, since they sink in sand and tar. (If you do have a side stand, you'll have to carry a board with you!)

- Equally useless is the average rear-view mirror that comes with the bike. If it's the kind that you can loosen with just a quick turn of the hand, have it replaced immediately with a good one—one that won't jiggle loose after twenty miles and then smash as it flies off onto the pavement.

- Although crash bars that protect your legs are sometimes called sissy bars, that's a misnomer. When you dump, you'll know why. Get them!

- The electric starter is worth every extra cent you pay for it. There's nothing worse than trying to kick-start a bike which is cold, wet, or overheated.

- Pay extra for a luggage rack.

Other motorcycling equipment

- Wear a helmet. The law requires it.

- A tinted bubble that covers your whole face is much better than goggles. Dust stings; bumblebees and fat bugs explode when they hit your face; and rain is unbearable at normal driving speeds (sixty to eighty miles per hour).

- Always carry spare spark plugs, since they foul constantly.

- Carry spare light bulbs.

- Use plastic laundry bags to protect the contents of your pack from getting soaked when it pours.
- Bring a pair of sunglasses with hardened lenses for low-speed driving.
- Bring or buy abroad hooked rubber straps to keep your pack from flying around.

Special clothing for motorcyclists

- Since bike-riding can be cold even on a summer night, think about bringing a down-filled parka or comparably warm jacket.
- Buy the best rain gear available, since you will be miserable if it leaks. It should snap closed around the sleeves and pant cuffs. Rain gear should be brightly colored (yellow or orange) to glow in the dark. Make it double as a windbreaker in clear weather.
- Bring heavy, comfortable boots. Combat boots work perfectly.
- Wear leather gloves, which will protect your hands from the cold and from the blisters you'll get as you work in the clutch and front brakes, which are always stiff on a new bike.

HITCHHIKING

Hitchhiking is known as **auto-stop** in Europe. It is accepted in some countries and loathed in others. The accompanying chart will give you a good idea of what success to expect in each country. (See also pp. 158-60.)

Advantages of hitchhiking

- Hitchhiking is as cheap as "free" can be. It offers total freedom—with one hitch: you've got to hitch a ride. So the only thing that can break down is you.
- Hitchhiking is also the best way to meet Europeans, because it's a direct and immediate appeal for help.
- Hitchhiking is a sport, and like all sports it reveals inner qualities in its participants. It's also an art, demanding skill, intelligence, and patience.

Disadvantages of hitchhiking

- Hitchhiking is time-consuming; tiring, very tiring; and potentially dangerous, especially for women traveling alone.
- Furthermore, it doesn't always work, as hitchhikers soon discover in southern Spain. You've got to be

tough, patient, and wily to make it work.

Prospects for Hitchhiking in European Countries

Austria . . . . Good.	**Liechtenstein** . . Does it matter?
Belgium . . . . Very good.	**Luxembourg** . . . Very good.
Denmark . . . . Excellent.	**Netherlands** . . . . Very good.
France . . . . The worst (especially in the south).	**Norway** . . . . Tough.
Germany . . . . Excellent.	**Portugal** . . . . Fair.
Great Britain . . . Excellent.	**Spain** . . . . Lousy.
Greece . . . . Poor.	**Sweden** . . . . Good.
Ireland . . . . Excellent.	**Switzerland** . . . . Good to very good.
Italy . . . . Good (despite hostility).	**Yugoslavia** . . . . . Fair, but getting worse.

Gear for hitchhikers

- Use backpacks with metal frames. They distribute the weight evenly, are great for walking, have convenient zippered compartments, take more abuse, don't get dirty quickly, and are harder to steal than most other packs.

- Or else use a pack made of leather and canvas. This kind takes up less space, rips less often, and never suffers from frame damage (because there is no frame to be damaged).

- Make sure the straps of the pack won't cut into your body or tear off. Check the stitching carefully.

- Bring a large poncho to cover both you and the pack in heavy rain.

- Pack a sleeping bag (down compresses the most, but comparable synthetics stay warmer when wet) and a thin foam pad.

- You'll also need a water container, a flashlight, some insect repellant, a Swiss Army knife, some soap in a plastic container, and matches.

- Carry most of your funds in traveler's checks or plan to use credit cards. Carrying cash is risky.

- You can buy gear abroad. Try Kaufman's (throughout Germany), Black's of Scotland (London), or Galleries LaFayette (Paris).

6
LODGINGS

Variety in places to stay—that's what Europe has to offer. And that's part of its charm and challenge to Americans not used to quite so diverse a choice.

VARIETIES OF LODGINGS

B & B (Bed and Breakfast) You'll find these small family hotels and boardinghouses throughout Great Britain. You'll get a comfortable, small room and usually a very good breakfast for a set price. They are usually inexpensive. You won't make reservations in most of these places. Look for "B & B" signs posted out front.

Boardinghouses Boardinghouses (**pensions, pensiones**) come in all categories, from luxurious to dismal, in every country in Europe. Generally, you rent a room without a bath. You eat in a central dining area. In some cases, you'll be expected to stay at least three days or so. The price you pay includes however many meals you agree to eat. Prices range from inexpensive to moderate. You normally don't make reservations for these accommodations.

Castle Hotels Many castles in France, Germany, and Great Britain have been converted into unusual hotels varying from ultradeluxe to quite uncomfortable. You can get information on castle (château) hotels from both the Austrian and French National Tourist Offices (see p. 23). A brochure is also available from Gast Im Schloss, D3526 Trendelburg 1, Germany. Lufthansa, the German airline, often stocks good brochures on castle hotels. The important thing to remember: both cost and comfort vary enormously among castle accommodations (some even serve as youth hostels).

Farmhouses These can be rented in Austria, Germany, and Ireland. For information, contact the appropriate national tourist office (see p. 23).

Historic Inns Great Britain is world-famous for its atmospheric inns, some dating back to medieval times. Comfort varies from inn to inn, but rates are uniformly reasonable. For a brochure and map, contact the British Tourist Authority. In Switzerland, you'll find many comparable historic inns, and a booklet will be sent to you free upon request from the Swiss National Tourist Office (see p. 23).

Home Exchange If you'd like to exchange your home with a foreign person, contact any of the following organizations: Vacation Exchange Club, 350 Broadway, New York, NY 10013; International Home Exchange, 503 D Street, San Rafael, CA 94901; Inquiline, 35 Adams Street, Suite 100, Bedford Hills, NY 10507.

Hotels Most tourist offices will send you booklets or pamphlets giving addresses and telephone numbers of hotels throughout each country. Note that they will contain no subjective comments, just facts on cost and conveniences. To come up with a good hotel, it's best to collect and cross-reference information from friends, guide books, and travel agents. (See also pp. 94-112).

Kroer A **Kro** (plural: **Kroer**) is a Danish country inn, often filled with the kind of atmosphere you'd travel thousands of miles to enjoy. And the food is often tops. These inns are quite expensive but still offer good value. You'll find them throughout the country. For a list of some of the most interesting, contact the Danish National Tourist Office (see p. 23).

Mission Hotels Throughout Scandinavia, the mission hotels offer modest, comfortable rooms at reasonable rates—reasonable for Scandinavia, that is. The only catch: no drinking is allowed. These hotels are very popular, and you'll want to reserve a room well in advance from May through September.

Paradores The Spanish government has supported the construction and maintenance of inns throughout Spain, some of which are starkly modern, while others are filled to the brim with native ambience. The **paradores** offer excellent value, comfortable rooms, and good regional cooking, and are located in areas of historic or cultural interest. Get a list from the Spanish National Tourist Office (see p. 23). Make reservations as far in advance as you can, especially during the peak season.

Pousadas Portugal's version of Spain's **paradores**, and very fine at that. Both countries have regulations on maximum stays, and you should make reservations as far in advance as possible. Even during the off season, the **pousadas** and **paradores** can be packed!

Private Homes Renting a room in a private home (**privat Zimmer, sobe**) can be a fascinating and relatively inexpensive experience. As you would guess, there are so many rooms available all over Europe that it's impossible to give any overall conclusion except for this: they usually give you good value, and people respond to you according to your warmth and openness.

If you'd like to stay in a private home in France or Great Britain, check into Chez des Amis, 139 West 87th Street, New York, NY 10024. This organization will introduce you to some interesting families. The cost is relatively high.

Pubs That's right. Throughout Great Britain and Ireland you can find rooms in pubs. Note that these have unusual hours, so that you can be locked out of your room unless you ask about closing times in advance. Fun, good value. Don't try to reserve such rooms in advance.

Relais de campagne These country inns offer excellent atmosphere, idyllic settings, comfort, and some of the best cooking in Europe. Most of them are located in France, but others are scattered in Belgium, Great Britain, Italy, and Sweden. For full information, contact the French National Tourist Office or call toll-free 800-221-4547 (Two World Tours, 245 Park Avenue, New York, NY 10017). Note that these are quite expensive, especially when it comes to quality cuisine.

Resorts Resorts vary just like hotels. You've got to check them out in advance. You'll need reservations during the peak season since all of Europe invades beach areas during hot summer weather.

Romantik Hotels A group of Austrian, German and Swiss hotels offering family-owned and operated inns to travelers. Each is atmospheric, comfortable, and reliable concerning its kitchen, which usually specializes in regional cooking. Many of these inns are located off-the-beaten-path for a true glimpse of another culture. Prices range from moderate to expensive, but are always good values. For information contact Lufthansa, the German airline, or the Germany National Tourist Office (see p. 23). You can also write directly to the central office of the group: Romantik Hotels and Restaurants, 8752 Gross-Weldheim, West Germany.

Rorbu Nothing more than fishing shanties, open to foreigners on the coast of Norway throughout the summer season. Cost varies from nothing to next to nothing. For the adventuresome. For information, contact the Norwegian National Tourist Office (see p. 23).

Student Hotels Don't confuse these with hostels. Student hotels are quite distinct. If you're a student or living on a student's budget, get in touch with the CIEE (see p. 16) for details on the assortment of student hotels and dorms in Europe.

Villas and Apartments You can rent apartments in the Algarve, Estoril (near Lisbon), London, Madrid, and Paris through Air India, British Airways, TWA, and Pan Am. Call the airlines for full information. Or contact: At Home Abroad, Inc., 136 East 57th Street, New York, NY 10022 or Vacation Exchange Club, 350 Broadway, New York, NY 10013. Most rentals are for a minimum of one week and include maid service.

Xenia These comfortable hotels are located throughout Greece and are supported in part by the government. For information on these fine hotels, contact the Greek National Tourist Office (see p. 23).

Youth Hostels Hosteling is one of the least expensive ways to get by in Europe. Very simple, modest, dormitory-style living, in most instances. For full information, contact American Youth Hostels, Delaplane, VA 22025. Or call any local branch for assistance.

YMCAs and YWCAs The Ys in Europe are much better than their counterparts in the U.S. and give you very good value for your travel dollars. For information, contact YMCA, 291 Broadway, New York, NY 10007; or YWCA, 600 Lexington Avenue, New York, NY 10022. Or call any local branch for assistance.

ROOM RESERVATIONS

Reservations are not necessarily essential for enjoyable travel, but they certainly can help, especially for brief trips. A poorly-made reservation may be worse than none at all, however. Here are some tips on doing it right.

When reserving a room makes sense

- Have a reservation for the first night abroad. Since you'll be exhausted when you arrive in Europe, you won't want to look for a room.

- Make reservations if you want rooms of great charm or value, especially during the peak season.

- If you're on a short trip with little time to waste, have reservations for every night abroad. You can't afford the hassle or the time involved in looking for rooms on your own.

Problems with reservations

- You may have to pay a fee for room reservations or else

foot the cost of cables and phone calls.

- You're usually renting sight unseen. Unless you have great confidence in your "source," you may end up disappointed.

- You'll end up paying for higher-priced rooms or paying the highest price a room will rent for. Reservations take away all your bargaining power and make it very difficult for you to shift from one room to another.

- Reservations tie you down. If you're on a short trip, this will make no difference, but when a trip stretches to three weeks or longer, a reservation schedule can begin to feel like an ill-fitting shoe on a ten-mile hike.

Avoiding getting bumped by hotels

Many hotels routinely overbook by 10 to 15 percent. Unless you've got a confirmation in writing, you could be one of those bumped.

- Make reservations as far in advance as possible. Note that some hotels in major cities fill up six to nine months in advance.

- Get your reservation confirmed in writing. If you know that you'll be arriving at a hotel after 6:00 p.m., make sure that the hotel knows this. And have this late arrival time noted on your room confirmation slip.

- Pay a substantial deposit on the room. With money in the bank, few hotels will worry about your showing up.

- If you make reservations through a travel agent, choose one with clout—preferably one with many offices abroad, so that you will have someone to call if things go awry.

- If you get delayed unexpectedly, notify the hotel. Few hotels will rent your room if you have contacted them.

Travel agents' reservations

- Most agents charge nothing at all for making room reservations, unless doing so involves a special service, such as phoning or cabling (their commission is paid by the hotel).

- Ask the agent whether you'll be charged for cables or phone calls—or for anything, for that matter!

- If the agent insists that there is no charge at all, ask whether a surcharge will be added to your hotel bill abroad.

- If the agent says that no such commission need be

paid, ask for a letter typed on the agency stationery stating this in straightforward terms. If a hotel in Europe then tries to stick you with a surcharge, produce the letter and refuse to pay it.

Airline reservation services

- With enough advance notice, airlines will gladly reserve a room for you at any destination or stopover point, both of which are stated clearly on your ticket. They charge no fee for this service.

Credit card reservations

- Note that with some credit cards you can get a confirmed room reservation in major hotels throughout Europe. Call major credit card companies for current information on making confirmed room reservations.

Making your own reservations

- Larger hotel chains with many branches abroad have toll-free (800) numbers listed in the phone book. All you have to do is dial the number and make a reservation. Be specific about dates and ask them to send you some sort of confirmation in writing. Also ask for a reservation or confirmation number.

- You can write to individual hotels listed in guide books, well ahead of time. State exact dates and details on the kind of room you'd like to have and the price you'd be willing to pay.

- Send your letter by airmail. Include international reply coupons (available in main post offices) to cover the cost of the hotel's airmail reply. (Tell the hotel to reply by airmail.)

- Most hotels will reply with a request for a deposit to show good faith. An international money order will do the trick. Sometimes just a check is good enough.

- Another method that's expensive but effective: call the foreign hotel during local business hours. Ask for the front desk, where you'll probably find someone who can speak English. Talk very slowly and very clearly. Repeat the dates of your intended stay several times. Ask for a written confirmation. And be sure to get the name of the person with whom you're talking.

Wiring for reservations

If you'd like to wire reservations abroad, it's easy and relatively inexpensive when you use the International Hotel Code. Note that this code is used neither in Great Britain nor in smaller, off-the-beaten-path hotels on the Continent. **Be sure to cancel reservations if it becomes necessary.**

- Find the hotel's telex address in its brochure and then choose your accommodations. Write your message out, complete with your name and address, before you send it.

- Request confirmation of your reservation. When it arrives, pack it with your travel documents. You'll want it with you to guarantee yourself a room when you get to the hotel.

International Hotel Code

(Please reserve:)

Single room and bed	**ALBA**
One room, double bed	**ALDUA**
One room, two beds	**ARAB**
One room, three beds	**ABEC**
Two single rooms	**BELAB**
Two rooms, three beds	**BIRAC**
Two rooms, two beds each	**BONAD**
Three single rooms	**CIROC**
Three rooms, four beds	**CARID**
Three rooms, five beds	**CALDE**
Three rooms, two beds each	**CADUF**
Four single rooms	**DANID**
Four rooms, two beds each	**DIROH**

(including)

Private bath	**BAT**
Sitting room	**SAL**
Ordinary garage	**GARAG**
Deluxe quality	**BEST**
Child's bed	**KIND**
Servant's room	**SERV**
Lock-up garage	**BOX**
Good view	**BELVU**
Good quality	**BON**
Simple quality	**PLAIN**
Very quiet	**TRANQ**
Facing courtyard	**INTER**
One night only	**PASS**
Staying several days	**STOP**

(arriving)

This morning	**POWYS**
This afternoon	**POZUM**
This evening	**RAMYK**
Tonight	**RAZEM**

	morning	afternoon	evening	night
Sunday	POBAB	POLYP	RABAL	RANUV
Monday	POCUN	POMEL	RACEX	RAPIN
Tuesday	PODYL	PONOW	RADOK	RAQAF
Wednesday	POGOK	POPUF	RAFYG	RATYZ
Thursday	POHIX	PORIK	RAGUB	RAVUP
Friday	POJAW	POSEV	RAHIV	RAWOW
Saturday	POKUZ	POVAH	RAJOD	RAXAB

Cancel....... **ANUL**

7

PACKING

What to take, how to pack it—some of the most basic questions of travelers! Read this chapter to simplify the process of finding answers. Then read through the "Travelers' Checklist" starting on page 71 to decide what to pack.

LUGGAGE VS. BAGGAGE

If you can't carry your luggage a mile without setting it down, it's too heavy. If you can't carry it on a plane as hand luggage, it's too large—it's what I call baggage. Baggage is burdensome, clumsy, and frustrating, and you don't need it! What you do need is good carry-on luggage. Mark it with colored tape so it's easy to spot.

Problems with baggage

- It costs you money at every turn (porters, extra taxi charges, etc.). You're forced to take taxis, so you miss savings on public transportation.

- It cuts your bargaining power at hotels. If you arrive with several bulky bags, you will be more apt to stay, no matter what the rates are. Clerks won't be as open to bargaining with you.

- It slows you down. You'll miss connections waiting for porters, checking and picking up checked baggage, or having to carry it yourself. And carrying baggage is hard work!

- It leaves you vulnerable. Carry-on bags can't get lost or misdirected, the way baggage can.

- It causes you undue worry. You have to check it or else keep a sharp eye on it whenever you're in transit. A carry-on bag can go with you—almost anywhere.

Carry-on bags

- Take no more than one small bag, which will serve as plane carry-on luggage.

- Try a canvas or vinyl bag, which will be relatively inexpensive, feather light, and soft-sided—avoid frames of any kind! You want a bag which is light, pliable, and durable.

- Get a bag with a shoulder strap, to make carrying easier. It should also have some small outer compartments for odds and ends, from toilet articles to an umbrella.

- Make sure it's stain-resistant and waterproof. Spray it with water-repellant if it's not.

Garment bags

If, no matter how hard you try, you can't get the things you'd like to take with you into one small bag, carry a garment bag onto the plane and hang it in one of the coat compartments.

- You'll pay half the price for the same bag if you shop for one in discount outlets. You can get a high-quality bag for around twenty dollars.

- Garment bags can also be made at home. Patterns appear in women's magazines and can be found in many fabric shops.

- The bag should have some outer pockets, again for odds and ends. These should have snap or zipper closings.

- It's much easier to carry the bag if it has a shoulder strap. Most do.

- Spray it with water-repellant to make sure it will be waterproof.

Weight restrictions

- Weight restrictions have been dropped on most airlines. Passengers are now limited to two bags with overall dimensions not exceeding 106 inches.

- Adding height, width, and depth, neither bag may exceed 62 inches.

- You'll pay a charge for any oversized baggage.

When you can't travel light

- Never carry one huge bag. Split the contents into two lighter bags for easier handling.

- Think about using a luggage roller. They do stick in cracks, but will make lugging baggage much easier, except on stairs.

- Think about taking a backpack. If you've ever worn one, you know how much easier it is than carrying a suitcase. No one will think you're crazy—just smart.

- Store your bags in lockers at airports and train stations whenever possible, to leave you free to do some sightseeing without dragging bags around with you.

- Remember that hotels will store bags if your flight or train leaves late at night, well past checkout time.

- Don't overpack! You can't collect insurance on baggage damages if your bags are really stuffed.

GENERAL PACKING TIPS

It's natural for you to feel somewhat skeptical about traveling with only one piece of carry-on luggage. Questions will pop into your mind: Can I really get by on only a few clothes? Won't I be embarrassed by wearing the same outfits over and over? Can I get by in formal places with less than very formal clothes? What do I do about climate changes? What happens if something gets stained? And so on.

If you choose your clothes wisely, you'll have no problem at all. I've traveled over a million miles in the last decade, always with no more than one bag that I could carry on a plane. The reaction to this style of travel has always been the same: are you ever smart! Finally, as long as you're clean and comfortably dressed, you'll exude an aura of contentment and confidence. And foreigners will judge you more by this attitude than by your clothes.

How to travel light

- Do it like the pros—stewardesses, travel writers, experienced businessmen, correspondents—and wear your heaviest clothes. Carry one other change of clothes on the plane. You can always pick up odds and ends abroad.

- Pack only items you need to survive—the essentials.

- Make each item serve as many purposes as possible. A bathing suit or bikini can pass as underwear. A one-piece woman's swimsuit can be converted into a dress by adding a wraparound skirt of the same material. Think versatility.

- Go for comfort first, style last. But the two need not be mutually exclusive.

- Make sure all clothes are light, easy to wash, and quick-drying. Test them before you leave.

- Spray water-repellant on any materials that are suited to such treatment (blouses, ties, jackets, etc.). This will help keep them clean.

Basics of packing

Use the rolling technique to keep clothes wrinkle-free and accessible in a small bag.

- Lay slacks out on a flat surface (such as a bed) with the leg seams together. These will serve as a base.

- Fold such things as T shirt, halter, sweater, turtleneck,

or shorts in half lengthwise, with sleeves together. Lay these out evenly on both the top and bottom portion of the slacks.

- Roll the stack of clothes into a loose ball, working from the pants legs up.

- You can just unroll the ball to get whatever item you need later on.

Packing garment bags

- Hang a number of clothes on no more than two hangers. If you use too many hangers, the bag will become bulky and overly heavy.

- Light plastic hangers with rounded corners work best. They don't rust and they help clothes keep their original shape.

- You can stuff an incredible number of small items into the bottom of a garment bag. The temptation to do so can result in a heavy bag!

Packing toiletries

- Put all liquids in plastic bottles. Place each bottle in a separate plastic bag, so that your bag won't get soaked if they leak.

- To prevent leaking: gently squeeze the bottle as you put the top on to create suction. Seal the top with tape for full protection.

- For long trips, take small bars of soap or sample-size bottles of toiletries. Plan to discard empties en route.

- As you use up your toothpaste and other creams in tubes, roll tubes up tightly so that they will take up less space.

- Since normal pill containers can pop open, spilling pills in all directions, don't take them. Put pills in the square metal containers for aspirin, which close tightly, take up very little space, and pack neatly into any bag. But carry prescriptions separately to avoid problems when going through customs.

- For pins, rubber bands, paper clips, and all small items, use hard matchboxes or empty film containers.

Companies specializing in travel items

You can buy travel odds and ends from the following companies that specialize in such merchandise: Henniker's, 779 Bush Street, San Francisco, CA 94120; Traveler's Checklist, Cornwall Bridge Road, Sharon, CT 06069; TravLTips Mart, Ltd., 40-21 Bell Boulevard, Bayside, NY 1136l.

Travelers' Checklist

A trip should start off relaxed, so pack well in advance of your departure. If you do, you will have a chance to check and recheck what's packed and to remember things you've overlooked.

Use this checklist to help you pack. It's an exhaustive list—but you should take only those things which will be essential to your enjoyment of a European trip.

☐ **Adaptor** Since currents vary from country to country, you'll need an adaptor to use with your electrical items. Adaptors are found in shops specializing in travel. My recommendation: do without electrical items completely!

☑ **Address book** Don't leave home without a small, light, thin address book to fill with the names of new acquaintances and to refer to if you write home. Absolutely invaluable! + Contacts at home

☐ **Alarm clock** Take one only if you have important meetings abroad and don't want to rely on hotel wakeup services (which is smart). You'll find tiny travel alarm clocks on the market.

☐ **Alcohol** Take a quart of your favorite brand into Scandinavia, where prices are exorbitant. Don't bother when going to other areas, unless you have a penchant for bourbon (a rarity abroad).

☑ **Antacid** Everyone should carry a few tablets. If you've got chronic problems, take all you could possibly need.

☑ **Aspirin** A must. Take along one of the small plastic or metal boxes that contain at least a dozen tablets. Or put some into a small, easy-to-carry pillbox.

☑ **Band-aids** Bring a few. They're light and take up little space.

☑ **Bathing suit** Bathing suits can double for underwear if they're easy to wash, quick-drying, light, and comfortable. Fifteen minutes in the sun is all it takes to dry out a suit after swimming or washing. If you're skeptical, test the idea before you start a trip. Pick suits that don't bind or have tight elastic belts.

For a bathing suit that can be converted into a dress by adding a wraparound skirt: McCall's Pattern No. 6337.

☐ **Bathrobe** Not essential and easily replaced by an overcoat. Leave it at home!

☐ **Belt** Men should bring one reversible or money belt. Women can easily replace belts with scarves, which are far more versatile and lightweight.

☐ **Birth certificate** Essential for long-term study abroad. It must be translated into the foreign language. A notarized copy will be helpful if you lose your passport.

☐ **Birth control pills** Bring extra, just in case you stay longer than you expect.

☐ **Black Tie** For the upper .1 percent (casino crowd).

☐ **Blazer** A great idea. It should be made of tightly woven material, stain- and wrinkle-resistant, and dark-colored. Spray it with water-repellant to prevent stains.

☑ **Blouse** Take two at most—one light-colored, one dark (or print). They should be light and easy to wash.

☐ **Boots** Bring either one pair of boots or one pair of shoes, but not both. They should be broken in and very comfortable. You can always buy beautiful boots and shoes abroad, if you run into a special occasion demanding elegant footwear!

☑ **Bottle opener** One of the most useful and easy-to-forget items! Get a Swiss Army knife with an opener on it.

☑ **Bra** Bring no more than two. Substitute a bikini top if possible.

☑ **Calamine lotion** Great for relieving the itching of insect bites and bee stings.

☑ **Camera and film** Great to have, but a hassle. Bring only if you're serious.

☐ **Camping carnet** Essential for campers (see p. 109).

☑ **Can opener** Absolutely essential, if you'll be shopping in grocery stores for picnics. Some Swiss Army knives come with these. Get a good one.

☐ **Cards, playing** Easy to forget, but a wonderful way to while away the hours on planes and trains.

☐ **Chapstick** Essential. The very things that cause chapped lips are also the most enjoyable: eating, drinking, kissing, and outdoor activities, all of which result in a loss of essential lip oils. Chapstick and tinted lipsticks with moisturizers contain both petroleum jelly and sunscreens to make them useful all year 'round.

☑ **Coats** Bring one only. (See **Raincoat, Trench coat, Overcoat,** and **Poncho.**)

☑ **Comb** Essential.

☐ **Corkscrew** Get a Swiss Army knife with one of these on it.

☑ **Credit cards** Increasingly helpful, with many travel advantages.

☐ **Cufflinks** Take shirts which don't require them. Just a nuisance.

☐ **Cummerbund** The same.

☐ **Curling iron** Can you get by without one? If not, make sure it's the lightweight, flat, plastic kind. (See **Adaptor.**)

☐ **Currency** Bring fifty dollars in small American bills to avoid the currency exchange rip-off. Carry only the amount of cash you can afford to lose.

☑ **Dental floss** Easy to forget. An unusual use: it cuts through cheese easily, making perfect thin strips for a picnic!

☑ **Deodorant** Take a small stick—not an aerosol can (such cans may explode on planes).

☐ **Desinex** Bring one small tube, if you're susceptible to athlete's foot.

☐ **Dinner jacket** Hardly a necessity for most travelers. A dark sports coat is usually acceptable attire even in stuffy places.

☐ **Dress** Take one at most. It should be wrinkle-resistant, easy to wash, and easy to dress up or down. Dresses of double-knit cotton T shirt material are excellent.

If the dress gets clingy on the trip, hang it in the bathroom while you take a shower or bath. The steam will be absorbed to prevent static electricity.

☐ **Dress shirt** Rarely needed and easily replaced with a nice white shirt.

☑ **Drugs** Take as many prescription drugs as you'll need for the entire length of the trip, plus enough for a week or two to spare. Carry prescriptions with you if you remove drugs from the original containers. And be sure to learn their generic names, in case you lose them.

☑ **Ear plugs** If you're sensitive to noise, these are just great on planes and in noisy hotels. Get the easy-to-mold kind, like Flents. I'd suggest that all travelers carry ear plugs, just in case.

☐ **Electric razor** No, don't take one. It's nothing but a hassle. Small, light travel kits consisting of a compact safety razor and blades make a lot more sense.

☐ **Eurailpass, BritRailpass** Remember that you can only buy these in the U.S. (see p. 49).

☐ **Evening bag** Not necessary, but nice at times. Maybe you should buy one abroad.

☐ **First-aid kit** Required for auto travel abroad (see p. 53).

☑ **Fish net shopping bag** Very smart to have. Light, compact, useful. Highly recommended.

☒ **Flag** A small one is useful for hitchhiking.

☑ **Flashlight** All motorists and travelers in Greece, Ireland, Portugal, and Yugoslavia should have one. So should campers in any country. Bring spare batteries.

☐ **Garters** Only if you can't do without.

☐ **Girdle** Likewise.

☐ **Glasses** One spare pair of both sunglasses and prescription glasses.

☐ **Gloves** Only when necessary, as for off-season travel and when traveling by motorcycle.

☑ **Hairbrush** Essential.

☐ **Hair dryer** Another gadget requiring an adaptor. Women for centuries got by without them. Can't you? (see **Adaptor**.)

☑ **Hair conditioner** If you use it, bring it with you, because it's hard to find in Europe. Make sure it's in a plastic container, tightly sealed, and placed in a plastic bag.

☐ **Hair spray** Get by without it, if possible. Take a small plastic container with pump, if not.

☐ **Halter** Useful as a T shirt or bra (or both).

☐ **Hankies** Use disposable tissues instead. Buy some as necessary in Europe.

☑ **Hat** Highly recommended is a cloth or khaki fisherman-style hat, deep enough to stay on your head in heavy winds with a wide brim to protect you from rain or sun. Spray it with water-repellant. It may be frumpy-looking, but it will do the job!

☐ **Health certificate** Needed only for extended foreign study. It must be translated into the foreign language.

☐ **Heater, immersible** A very clever gadget that heats up water quickly, but needed only for long-term travel. You can usually get water hot enough for tea or hot chocolate by letting the faucet run. (See **Adaptor**.)

☐ **Helmet** Required of motorcyclists, who'll get fined for disobeying the law if they don't wear them. Get a helmet with a bubble to protect your face from rain, sleet, and bugs.

☑ **Hostel card** All hostelers should have one (see p. 108).

☑ **Insect repellant** Only necessary for campers and ardent bathers. Get the strongest stuff available, in small plastic containers.

☑ **International driver's license** Don't leave home without one if you intend to drive in Europe (see p. 15).

☐ **International student identification card** Every student should take along one of these for travel in Europe (see p. 16).

☐ **Iron** Don't bring one. Instead, take clothes that are wrinkle-resistant or wrinkle-proof.

☐ **Jacket** Fine for casual travel, but don't bring one if you're taking an overcoat.

☑ **Jeans** Accepted almost everywhere, even in sophisticated places. Europe has gone casual, imitating the millions of youthful American vagabonds. Simple is best, and jeans typify the trend.

Jeans make excellent ski pants if you spray them with water-repellant.

☐ **Jewelry** Leave it at home. Or wear simple, all-purpose jewelry that you'll never take off. Scarves are much better and more versatile as a way of adding fantasy to your wardrobe.

☑ **Knapsack** One of the smartest ways of carrying weight, if you can't force yourself to travel light. Also a very good item for trekking. Only in the more expensive hotels would knapsacks be frowned upon.

☑ **Knife** Essential. Get a good Swiss Army knife with a bottle opener, can opener, corkscrew, scissors and tweezers.

☐ **Laces** Change the laces on your shoes or boots before going to Europe. This way you won't have to take a spare set along.

☑ **Laundry soap** Get a few travel packets.

☐ **Lighter** Take one if needed. Or take several. Lighters make great gifts, especially in Portugal.

☐ **Lomotil** A very strong medicine that works wonders for diarrhea and requires a prescription from your doctor. Get some and bring it!

☐ **Magic marker** Ideal for making signs if you'll be hitchhiking. It should be permanent ink, which won't run in the rain.

☑ **Maps** Get the best available, in a light and easy-to-handle form. Free maps are sent out by tourist offices. If you're a member of travel or auto clubs, they'll often provide maps free of charge. Highly detailed maps are available in bookstores abroad.

☑ **Mirror** One tiny pocket mirror is enough.

☐ **Money clip** Not necessary and a come-on to crooks.

☑ **Nail clippers** Easy to carry and worth bringing.

☐ **Nail file** The same.

☐ **Nail polish and remover** Can you get by without it? If not, be sure to put polish in a plastic bag. You may want to seal the bottle with candle wax. It's simply disastrous when polish leaks on your clothes.

You can use a dab of polish to stop runs in hose.

☐ **Nasal spray** Particularly for hay-fever victims.

☐ **Needle and thread** Bring one needle and a little thread (off the spool). If you have trouble threading the needle, dip the thread in nail polish. To shield the point, poke the needle into half a dozen twist ties from a package of plastic bags. Fold the twist ties around the point. Wrap the thread around the outside. You'll also find many uses for the twist ties during your trip.

☐ **Nightgown** Almost all experienced women travelers replace a nightgown with a T shirt.

☐ **Nylons** Bring no more than two pairs of nylons or kneehighs per travel week. If nylons get baggy, just dip your hands in warm water and rub them from the ankles up.

To stop a run: use a dab of nail polish.

In desperation: if the opposite legs of two pairs of panty hose have been damaged, cut them off. Then wear both as if they were one pair.

☐ **Overcoat** If you take an overcoat, get one made of any tightly woven material that doesn't pick up lint, doesn't stain easily, and doesn't wrinkle. Take one coat that best matches your style of travel. Spray the coat with water-repellant so that it can double for a raincoat; it can also be used as a bathrobe when you trip down the hall to take a bath. It also makes a good blanket in a freezing train compartment. Button it loosely around yourself like a straitjacket: this will trap your body heat and keep you warm.

You may want to have a buttondown flap or zipper sewn on the inside pocket. This will protect anything placed there from pickpockets and keep things from falling out accidentally. You may also want to sew in extra pockets—a very simple technique to increase what you can carry on your body.

☐ **Pajamas** Totally unnecessary. It's this kind of thing that's got to go if you're going to travel light.

☐ **Panties** You can substitute a bathing suit for one pair. Since they're so light, you can bring several pairs—all nylon for fast drying.

☐ **Pants** Don't carry more than two pairs, one of which should be jeans. The other pair should be easy to wash and dark-colored to hide stains.

☐ **Paper clips** Bring a few. If you have a visa, place a clip on that page of your passport to make it easy to find.

☐ **Passport** If you forget this, forget the trip. **Carry your passport with you at all times and guard it with everything but your life!** You'll need it when exchanging currency, cashing traveler's checks, picking up mail at **poste restante** (general delivery) or at American Express, signing in at the hotel, and whenever the police ask to see it. If you're involved in a traffic accident abroad and are not carrying your passport, you may end up in the clink.

☐ **Passport wallet** A good way to carry a passport, currency, credit cards, papers, etc.

☐ **Pen** One of the most useful items abroad. Bring one or two.

☐ **Photos** Photomat photos can be used in a number of ways—for an international driver's license, for study abroad (identification papers), ski-lift passes, etc. It's a good idea to carry a few extras.

☐ **Plastic bags** Bring along the size and number appropriate to your style of travel. Possible uses: to hold bottles containing liquids, to carry soiled or damp clothes (such as a swimsuit), to protect clothes from the rain (as in backpacking), to sit on at picnics or spectator sports, to hold food in a car (plastic keeps banana and cheese odors contained).

☐ **Plastic flask** A gem, to be filled with water, booze, fruit juice, or whatever. Great for long plane rides when you don't want to rely on the whim of a stewardess, and especially good for car and train travel. Also a good way to avoid the high liquor prices in hotels (who doesn't drink in a room these days?). Don't leave home without one or two flasks!

☐ **Poncho** Although this is a good replacement for an overcoat, the latter will prove more versatile.

Purse   Don't be timid! Carry a huge purse with room to spare. Forget about style. It should have tight-fitting clasps to prevent spills and thwart thieves.

Within a larger purse you can use smaller cosmetic cases for odds and ends. This keeps things from getting jumbled together in one large mess.

☐   **Radio**   Leave it at home. If that's not possible, bring a minuscule transistor radio with a few spare batteries. Sell it before returning home. Every maid you meet will want it. Do not play your radio on a plane, because it can interfere with instruments!

☐   **Raincoat**   Replace this with a trench coat or overcoat, both of which can be sprayed with water-repellant. plastic pocket bag

☐   **Rain gear**   Essential for backpackers, hitchhikers, and motorcyclists. Get the best money can buy with rugged seams, snap-tight cuffs, and a durable hood.

☐   **Razor**   Take one with a few extra blades. Minuscule travel kits are on the market.

☐   **Rollers**   Can you make it without them? Can you change your hair style to make them unnecessary? If your hair gets a little messy, use the standby technique of covering it with a scarf. If you do bring rollers, here's a tip for a quick set: roll dry hair, cover with damp towel for five minutes, remove it, and let hair dry.

You can get free or inexpensive washes and sets in many foreign beauty schools. Ask the concierge to look them up in the foreign telephone book.

☐   **Rubber baggage tie-down straps**   The best way to hold gear on a motorcycle.

Rubber or nylon braided clothesline   Inexpensive, light, and useful. Great for hanging up wet clothes in limited spaces.

A note: never let foreign maids see them, or they'll take them from you. Technically, you're not supposed to do laundry in hotel rooms (but everyone does).

Safety pins   Bring a few. Use them to keep your pockets closed to protect your wallet.

☐   **Sandals**   Buy an inexpensive pair abroad when needed.

☐   **Sanitary products**   Take tampons and a few minipads. Also available in Europe at pharmacies.

☐   **Scarves**   Just like gold to women travelers, because they're stylish, lightweight, compact, and versatile (they can be used as belts, skirts, and even shawls). Scarves replace jewelry, transforming one outfit into many.

You must cover your head with a scarf in most Roman Catholic churches in Europe.

☐   **School transcript**   Students wishing to study abroad must have a school transcript with seal imprinted on it. It must be translated into the foreign language.

☐   **Scissors**   The small travel scissors prove useful, but are not indispensable.

Seeds   You may think this item's for the birds, but packaged flower seeds from home make a great gift, a wonderful way to say thanks to a foreign host. Since they're lightweight and easy to carry, think about bringing some.

Shampoo   Bring as little as you can get by with—in a plastic container.

☐   **Shirt**   Two at most. They should be easy to wash and dry. Dark colors are best.

Shoes   Take one pair of your most comfortable walking shoes. Don't bring shoes that need polishing. You don't want to worry constantly about how they look, and you want to avoid the hassle of having shoeshine boys tagging along behind you.

You can replace shoes with boots, but don't take both. Make sure they're comfortable.

Women's shoes should be comfortable and durable. Do not worry about how they look. When you travel, you can overlook style. If you need an elegant pair of shoes for a special occasion, buy a pair in Europe.

Do not wear high heels. Much of the enjoyment of travel comes from walking ancient streets and visiting hard-to-reach sights. High, thin heels are forbidden in many museums and castles, because they damage the floors!

☐ **Shoe polish**   If you follow the advice under **Shoes**, this becomes an unnecessary item.

☑ **Shorts**   Replace with a bathing suit in resort areas. Elsewhere, put on pants, skirt, or dress. In Europe, shorts are for tennis courts only.

☐ **Shower cap**   If needed, get the light plastic kind found in hotel rooms. It scrunches down to nothing. On the other hand, you can wrap your head in a towel like a turban and do without a cap.

☐ **Ski jacket**   A good replacement for an overcoat if you'll be hitch-hiking, skiing, or cycling. Make sure it's down-filled or made with top-quality down substitute (like Polargard).

☐ **Skirt**   Bring one at the most. It must be easy to wash, dark-colored to hide stains, and wrinkle-resistant.

A long print skirt with a drawstring or elastic waist can be worn higher, like a muu-muu. And it makes a nice bathrobe. Create one yourself from Butterick Pattern No. 5387. For a skirt-dress combination, try Butterick Pattern No. 6140.

☐ **Slacks**   You need no more than one pair. Some come with drawstrings—very useful for fluctuating weight!

☐ **Sleeping bag**   If you'll be camping out, get the best you can afford. A bulky item that should be carried only if necessary.

☐ **Sleeping pills**   Get a few from your doctor to help out with jeg lag.

☐ **Sleeping sheet**   Required in hostels. You can make or buy one (see p. 000).

☐ **Slippers**   Unnecessary. If you disagree, get the fabric kind that fold into a tiny package.

☐ **Slip**   No more than one, if any at all.

☐ **Soap**   Take small, individually wrapped bars—the kind you find in hotels. Tuck them into a plastic soap dish. Some hotels offer soap, some don't.

Liquid soap may be more manageable than bars and can be found in plastic containers. In a pinch, use shampoo or shaving cream for soap: both work well.

Empty film containers with rubber tops make excellent containers for powdered soap and detergent.

☑ **Socks**   One pair to wear and one for a spare—of synthetic material. Both wool and cotton hold up well, but are difficult to wash and take a long time to dry. That's why synthetics are better for travel.

Many hotels do not have stoppers in the sink. A sock works well as a replacement.

To wash socks quickly: put them on your hands like surgeon's gloves and scrub them with a bar of soap.

☐ **Spare keys**   All motorists should have one set of spare keys, best stored in a small magnetic box that can be hidden anywhere on the car.

☐ **Sports coat**   Only necessary if you plan to dress up occasionally—that is, if you'll be staying in nicer hotels and going to fancier restaurants. Take one that's lightweight, but not a wash-and-wear jacket, which will end up looking like a used handkerchief after two days.

Tweed is one of the better materials, because it's tough and rarely looks like it needs cleaning, even if it really does. Corduroy's OK. So are some double knits.

Choose a dark color. It's going to be stained at some time during the trip, so let the stains disappear in a dark brown or blue sea of color. Spray the coat with water-repellant. You'll get rained on for sure, and the repellant will fend off dirt as well.

The inside pocket should have a button-down flap or a zipper to lock in its contents. This can be added at home or inexpensively at a dry cleaner's specializing in simple garment repairs and alterations. If you forget to have this done, use a safety pin to fasten the top of the pocket.

☐ **Spot remover** This should be unnecessary if you travel with easy-to-wash clothes.

☐ **Stamps** Colorful American stamps—the lightest, least expensive, most appreciated, simplest gift to carry for foreigners you meet.

☐ **Stole** Another .1 percent item.

☐ **Studs** The same.

☐ **Suit** Unnecessary, except when on business trips. An attractive sports coat can replace a suit almost everywhere.

☑ **Suntan lotion** If needed, bring one small plastic bottle or buy some in Europe.

☑ **Sweater** One at most, none if possible. If you take one, wear it, to save precious packing space.

☐ **Tape** Occasionally helpful, but not indispensable.

☐ **Tent** If you'll be camping out, bring a light one. And be sure to try it out before taking it to Europe.

☑ **Tickets** Easy to forget, but don't!

☐ **Tie** One at most. Spray it with water-repellant. This will make it easy to remove any stains!

☑ **Toilet paper** Tuck a small wad into your purse or wallet. Refill as necessary. This may seem comical, but it isn't, as you will find out.

☑ **Toothbrush and paste** Bring a small tube and replenish as needed.

☐ **Towel** A real hassle to carry, but many European hotels give you miniature versions of the real thing.

☐ **Tranquilizers** Get a few from your doctor, just in case.

☑ **Traveler's checks** Most money should be carried in this form (see p. 16).

☐ **Trench coat** Take either one trench coat or one overcoat—but don't take them both. Trench coats should have removable linings. These linings make good pillows.

If your coat has a flimsy pocket, replace it with a deep and solid one. This will give you added space and protection. The pocket should have a button-down flap or a zipper. Add extra pockets, if you have the time. They'll come in handy.

And be sure to spray the coat with water-repellant, which will protect it from stains and rain.

☐ **Triangle danger sign** Required by law for motorists in Europe (see p. 53).

☑ **T shirt** You'll probably live in it. You can also sleep in it.

☐ **Tucks** Available at drugstores, Tucks will be of interest to hemorrhoid sufferers.

☐ **Turtlenecks** Not recommended, because they're hard to wash and dry slowly. However, they do not wrinkle.

☐ **Tweezers** A good little item, which takes up very little space and often comes in handy. Some Swiss Army knives have tweezers on them.

☑ **Umbrella** Bring one that folds down to less than fourteen inches long. If you shop around, you'll find one for a steal. Put the umbrella in one of the outside pockets of your carry-on bag.

☑ **Underwear** Use the new, synthetic-fiber underwear: easy to wash, quick-drying, and very colorful. Underwear can easily be replaced by bathing suits.

☐ **Visas** Necessary for long-term study abroad and for travel in Eastern European countries (see p. 12).

☐ **Washcloth** Do they exist in Europe? If you must have one, bring it along!

☐ **Watch** Toothpaste will help clean a fuzzy crystal.

☑ **Wet Ones** These pre-moistened cloths, available in drugstores, are not necessary, but are nice.

☑ **Windbreaker** Good in the Mediterranean areas and anywhere along the Atlantic. Can be used in place of a shirt. Or simply buy what's known as a wind shirt.

☐ **Woolite** Bring a few travel packets, if you have any woolen items along.

8

FINAL STEPS

Few travel books will tell you about steps you can take to give yourself peace of mind while away from your home or apartment. An important part of the relaxation you deserve on a vacation depends upon these precautions. With over 2 million burglaries a year in the U.S., it's a reasonable concern.

Home Security Checklist

- Cover or screen garage windows, so that a potential burglar will not know if your cars are gone.
- If your tools are normally in the garage, bring them inside.
- Put valuables and important documents in a safety deposit box.
- Never talk about upcoming trips with strangers.
- Get an engraving pen and I.D. number from the local police to mark your valuables. Put "Operation Identification" stickers on doors and windows.
- Make sure basement windows are locked or protected with grilles.
- Place removable drop bars on sliding glass doors.
- Never leave spare keys in their "secret" hiding place while you're gone.
- If you leave your car at an airport parking lot while you're away, don't leave a house key on your car keychain.
- Set the bell of your telephone at its lowest ring, so that any potential burglar will not hear it go unanswered from outside the house or apartment. If you have plug-in style phones, unplug them for the same reason.
- Leave window shades and blinds in different positions, the way you would if you were at home.
- Get the post office and newspaper to stop delivery a day before you leave.
- Ask a neighbor to pick up any letters, packages, or papers that may get through.
- Have a lawn boy continue to keep up your garden and lawn.
- Ask your neighbor to park his car in your driveway — occasionally.
- Have him fill up a garbage can or two with his trash from time to time.
- If your trip has been announced for any reason in a local paper, hire a house sitter. Burglars use these announcements as one of their main sources of information.
- Never leave notes outside the house.
- Steal the most valuable items from a potential thief by carting TVs, radios, stereos, guns, and so on, to the house of a neighbor or friend.
- Make sure your insurance policy is paid for and up to date.

PLANT CARE WHILE YOU'RE GONE

No one wants to spend weeks, months, or years growing

beautiful house plants, only to return to a withered mass of brown mold or leafy splinters. To avoid these losses, use a plant sitter, especially if you'll be gone three weeks or longer.

Using a plant sitter

- Give the sitter a key and basic instructions on care.

- Put an identifying mark or a reminder note on each plant needing special care (misting, infrequent watering, etc.).

Doing without a plant sitter

If you'll be gone less than three weeks, you can get by without a plant sitter.

- Remove all dead leaves, flowers, and buds.

- Place a plastic bag on the bottom of your tub and cover it with several layers of newspaper.

- Spray the paper with water until it's thoroughly moist.

- Cover the paper with another sheet of plastic and sprinkle it with water as well.

- Soak plants thoroughly, allowing excess water to drain completely before setting them on the plastic.

- When all your plants are in the tub, cover them with a plastic sheet and tape it in place. Poke some holes in it to let air circulate.

- Leave the bathroom shades up (or turn on the light if there are no windows).

- If you have more plants than your tub holds, or in the case of huge plants, group them away from direct sunlight and follow the same general procedure to trap humidity after a thorough soaking and draining. Poke holes in your plastic coverings to ventilate plants.

THE LAST FEW DAYS

The way you handle the minor details of any trip in the last few days before going abroad could make a major difference in averting problems.

Three days before your flight

- Reconfirm your flight reservation, according to the procedure outlined on your ticket.

- Get the name of the person you are speaking to and note the day and time you call.

- If you should get bumped from your flight, this procedure gives you grounds for legal action.

- More important, this call will usually drastically lower the odds of your being bumped at all.

The day before your flight

- Check to make sure no mail or papers are delivered.

- Take the pets to the place where they'll be staying.

- Check through the things you'll be taking (see pp. 71-77).

- Make a list of what's in each bag. If a bag gets lost, you'll be able to identify its contents exactly. When the bag is opened after three days, you and it can be reunited quickly.

The day of your flight

- Call the airport to ask whether your flight will be leaving on time. If you are a member of a tour, you'll usually be informed about any delays, but if you are an individual traveler, this would be rare indeed.

- Turn down the heat in your house (if it's possible).

- Water the plants for the last time.

- Make sure the house is secure, all windows and doors locked.

Getting to the airport

- Figure out how long it takes to get to the airport. Then allow an extra forty-five minutes for delays and traffic jams.

- Add another half-hour for Friday and Sunday nights or for either Los Angeles International or New York's JFK.

- Now add another hour if you intend to register items with customs (see p. 82).

- To avoid the congestion around the terminal, park in one of the more remote parking lots. If you are traveling light, you won't mind the walk!

AT THE AIRPORT

All you want to do is to get to the airport, check your luggage, walk through the security check, and board the plane with the minimum of delay and hassle. Today, that's asking quite a lot.

beautiful house plants, only to return to a withered mass ᴜ mold or leafy splinters. To avoid these losses, use a plant especially if you'll be gone three weeks or longer.

Using a plant sitter

- Give the sitter a key and basic instructions on care.

- Put an identifying mark or a reminder note on each plant needing special care (misting, infrequent watering, etc.).

Doing without a plant sitter

If you'll be gone less than three weeks, you can get by without a plant sitter.

- Remove all dead leaves, flowers, and buds.

- Place a plastic bag on the bottom of your tub and cover it with several layers of newspaper.

- Spray the paper with water until it's thoroughly moist.

- Cover the paper with another sheet of plastic and sprinkle it with water as well.

- Soak plants thoroughly, allowing excess water to drain completely before setting them on the plastic.

- When all your plants are in the tub, cover them with a plastic sheet and tape it in place. Poke some holes in it to let air circulate.

- Leave the bathroom shades up (or turn on the light if there are no windows).

- If you have more plants than your tub holds, or in the case of huge plants, group them away from direct sunlight and follow the same general procedure to trap humidity after a thorough soaking and draining. Poke holes in your plastic coverings to ventilate plants.

THE LAST FEW DAYS

The way you handle the minor details of any trip in the last few days before going abroad could make a major difference in averting problems.

Three days before your flight

- Reconfirm your flight reservation, according to the procedure outlined on your ticket.

- Get the name of the person you are speaking to and note the day and time you call.

Registering valuables

It's best to register valuable items before you get to the airport, but if you forgot, do it now. Otherwise, when you come back to the U.S., you may have to pay duty on items that you did not actually purchase in Europe.

- You'll find registration booths in international airports as a part of the Customs Department.

- You'll be asked to fill out a small white form with pertinent information, including a description of the article and serial numbers when applicable. **You must have the items with you in order to register them!** The official will check over the information, verify it, stamp the form, and give it to you as proof that you had these items before going abroad. The slip is valid for all future trips, so don't throw it away.

- If you have items to register, allow yourself an extra hour for the process. Occasionally, the booths are closed—it's inexcusable, but true.

Boarding a plane

It all used to be so simple. All you had to do was tie a string on your finger and point yourself toward the plane. It's not quite so easy nowadays. To get on to a plane, you need a ticket, a boarding pass, and in most cases a seat-selection card.

- If you don't have your ticket yet, you'll wait in line.

- If you have to check baggage, you'll wait in line.

- However, with a ticket in hand and bags either with you or checked, you can proceed straight to the boarding gate. If you arrive too late, you may lose your seat.

Security and customs

To get to the gate, you'll have to pass through a security check. In a crowded airport, this can take forty-five minutes or longer.

- If it's obvious that you're in danger of missing your plane, go right to the front of the line and calmly explain your predicament to security personnel.

- Under no circumstances should you make joking remarks about hijacking or bombs!

- If you get hassled for carrying a Swiss Army knife, have them put it in a package to be given to the stewardess on your flight. If they refuse this courtesy, have them put it in an envelope to be sent to your home.

- On some international flights, you'll pass through a

customs inspection, which may add another thirty minutes' delay. So start for the gate as soon as possible.

At the boarding area

- Unless you already have a seat assignment and boarding pass, you'll wait in line at the counter at the boarding area. You'll be given both at this time.

- Until you have a boarding pass in your hand, you essentially have nothing—except a contract that gives you specific legal rights. In short, you can still be bumped.

- When the plane is ready for boarding, the flight will be announced. If you do not board the plane when you're supposed to, your seat can be given to a standby.

Seat assignments

- Ask for a seat away from the galleys, partitions, or toilets.

- Choose an aisle seat if you have long legs. If not, choose a window seat.

- If you are traveling with one other person, reserve the window and aisle seats in a three-seat section. Few people select middle seats unless a plane is fully booked. If someone should sit down there, just switch seats with him so that you and your friend can sit together. If no one shows up, it will be easy for one of you to find a single seat while the other person sleeps. This way you can guarantee yourself at least a few hours of slumber.

- Find out whether there are any infants traveling on your flight. Stewardesses like to seat parents with young children in the first row of seats behind the partition nearest the galley; so if you relish peace and quiet on a long flight, choose a seat far enough away from that first row.

- If you're traveling alone, be the last person to board. Look for a block of three unoccupied seats. If you board late enough, most stewardesses will allow you to sit anywhere.

- If they go by the book and force you to take an assigned seat, agree. You can move as soon as the cabin door is locked.

PROBLEMS WITH FLIGHTS

This section gives you information about problems that you may run into when flying and strategies to help you cope with them.

Lost airline tickets

- Whenever you buy an airline ticket, write down the ticket number, date and place of purchase, and method of payment. Carry this information separately from your ticket—perhaps on the same piece of paper as your list of traveler's check numbers.

- If you lose a ticket or have one stolen, **immediately** go to or call the refund department of the airline from which you bought the ticket. You'll be asked to fill out a refund application.

- If you want to replace the ticket, you'll have to buy a new one, using the original form of payment. (If you paid for the original ticket with a credit card, your account can be credited immediately for the lost or stolen ticket. If you paid with cash or by check, you will be reimbursed only after a 120-day waiting period. This is one big advantage of using credit cards!)

- You're liable for the loss should the ticket be used illegally during the 120-day waiting period.

- You may be given a card to send in for a refund after the waiting period is over. If you don't send it in, you will not get the refund.

- In short, treat airline tickets like cash and expect nothing but grief if you lose one!

Getting bumped by airlines

Your plane ticket is a legal contract with an airline. It guarantees your right to the flight, under specific conditions.

- An international ticket is valid only if you reconfirm your flight within seventy-two hours of departure. Always get the agent's name when you reconfirm a flight.

- You must arrive at the airport within the time limit specified on your ticket. If you do not confirm your flight or if you arrive late, the airline can sell your seat to another person (bump you from the flight)—legally! If you do reconfirm your flight and arrive on time, the airline cannot legally sell your seat. However, airlines do so—about 150,000 times a year.

Voluntary and involuntary bumping

Nowadays airlines ask for volunteers to be bumped for a sum of money that varies with each airline and situation. If there are not enough volunteers, then some people will be bumped involuntarily. This could include you.

- If this happens to you, ask for the written statement

outlining compensation for being denied boarding. Depending upon the value of your ticket, you'll be paid a minimum of $37.50 to a maximum of $200.00 as denied boarding compensation (DBC). This money is yours for the inconvenience caused you by having been bumped.

- Note that DBC is only paid to passengers bumped from flights that actually take place (not canceled or delayed flights). It's meant only to discourage overbooking, which airlines do to survive.

- If an airline cannot get you to your original destination within two hours of the original scheduled arrival time for a domestic flight, or within four hours for an international flight, the DBC must be doubled, and the airline still must get you to your destination.

- Note that foreign airlines may not accept these rules for flights originating outside the United States.

Taking it to court

You are under no obligation to accept DBC, since you can take the matter to civil court. The odds are against you there, however. And it's an unbelievable hassle.

- Don't accept DBC if you plan to take your case to court. Once you accept the compensation, the affair is closed. You have no further legal redress.

- Be sure you have a case before you act. The airline does **not** have to pay DBC if the government takes over a plane (very rare), if a smaller plane is substituted for the original aircraft (occasionally happens), if you have not reconfirmed your flight, or if you check in later than the time specified on your ticket.

Consumer protection agencies

- If you really get into a jam, contact the Air Travel Consumer Protection Bureau, 90 Church Street, New York, NY 10007, (212) 264-1700. Or call any of its branch offices—in Chicago, (312) 694-2686; Dallas-Fort Worth Airport, (817) 429-0951; Los Angeles, (213) 536-6297; Miami, (305) 526-2535; or Seattle, (206) 764-3587.

- You can make complaints to the Civil Aeronautics Board, 1825 Connecticut Avenue, N.W., Washington, DC 20428.

- Naturally, it's to your advantage to work out all problems with the airline on a fair, even-handed basis.

Changes of fares

Once you have paid for and received a ticket, you cannot be

charged more money to board a plane within the U.S. However, in Europe you may be forced to pay whatever fare is applicable on that day.

- Note that Pan Am guarantees its fares anywhere.

- Be sure to ask the airline what its policy is when purchasing a ticket for international flights.

Flight delays

- When a flight is delayed after initial boarding has started, the airline is obligated to provide meals, lodging, transportation, and a free phone call to each passenger.

- If you have not started to board a plane and a delay is announced, you have no legal right to demand compensation of any kind. Nevertheless, most airlines will provide necessary amenities to stranded passengers.

- You will usually be given a voucher for a set-price meal and, in extreme cases, even a free hotel room.

- If the airline does not volunteer such things, don't hesitate to ask—and be polite, firm, and fair in your request.

Changing travel dates

Most discounted tickets require passengers to fly within specific time periods, with no changes allowed. If you try to make a change, the airline may ask you to pay full fare. This rule can be overriden for humanitarian reasons, and it's up to the airline to decide what that means in a given case.

- Note that you can take out special insurance to cover changes in travel plans caused by illness or death in the family.

In-flight precautions

- Never leave money, valuable papers, or your passport unattended at any moment on a plane. They should be carried on your person at all times—even when you go to the bathroom! And this advice goes double for when you get off the plane during a stopover.

- Get up and stretch occasionally; it will keep your body relaxed.

- Water and juice served on board will not be enough fluid to prevent dehydration, which is one of the factors leading to jet lag. Bring a flask or bottle of cold water or juice to drink on the flight. (The water on board is usually lukewarm.)

Jet lag

When people cross a number of time zones, they experience something known as jet lag. The condition, a foul-up of the natural body rhythms, varies from mild to dangerous, depending upon the person and his physical condition. People with strong internal clocks (who wake up at exactly the same time each morning without an alarm) tend to have marked jeg lag.

- Any person fifty or older who has diabetes, high blood pressure, or either pulmonary or arterial problems, should consult a doctor before crossing many time zones. Jet lag has recently been linked to heart attacks.

- Jeg lag symptoms: fatigue, irritability, anxiety, headaches, insomnia, and hunger in the middle of the night.

Avoiding jet lag

- Go to bed early for three or four days before flying abroad. This will prepare your body for the time change to come.

- Don't make a marathon of any trip. Break long trips into smaller segments, taking advantage of stopover opportunities.

- A simple solution: take a morning flight abroad, which will allow you to recoup in about twelve hours. Night flights are more exhausting and require about twenty-four hours of cold storage (according to doctors).

- If possible, take a weekend flight, and allow for one day of rest.

- Drink lots of nonalcoholic fluids to reduce the effects of jet lag.

Strategies for night flights

- If you have to fly at night, sleep through the entire trip. If you have to take a sleeping pill, do it. Don't try booze—martini poisoning combined with jet lag can be lethal (almost).

- Use pillows and blankets (in the compartment above your seat) to get comfortable and warm.

- Take off your shoes and loosen all tight-fitting clothing.

- Use ear plugs and eye masks. (Who cares what you look like? They work!)

- Draw the shades and tell the stewardess not to bother you, not even for snacks and meals.

- If you can't sleep, go easy on food.

Once you arrive

On arriving in Europe, plan to go right to bed, even if it's still light out. Get as much sleep as you can without worrying about getting in tune with the new time schedule.

- If that's impossible, at least go to bed early.

- Eat sparingly for two days as your body becomes accustomed to new meal times.

- Businessmen should never rush off to meetings without enough rest to get them physically and mentally prepared for tough decisions.

Part II: The Trip

9

ARRIVING IN EUROPE

It's a fairly straightforward process getting from the airport to the hotel, but things can and do go wrong. The hints in this section deal with customs, obtaining foreign currency, handling luggage, and finding a way to your hotel.

FOREIGN CUSTOMS AND CURRENCY EXCHANGES

Most people are a little bit nervous going through customs, and that's natural. However, anyone who seems overly nervous or who makes jokes may find himself going through a customs check.

In some airports you'll find two gates set aside for incoming passengers. One is marked "Nothing to declare." Naturally, if you have nothing to declare, you simply walk through the gate and out to the real world. Of course, you can still be stopped for a spot check. But normally a person carrying very little baggage sails through customs!

Common customs questions

- Never volunteer information while going through customs! You'll seem suspicious if you do.

- Customs officials can ask you to tell them the exact amount of money you're bringing in and in what form you've got it. If you're low on money, tell them you plan to stay only a week or so in the country, and that you plan to stay with a friend (have a name and address ready). But only say these things if they ask.

- Always tell officials that your reason for travel is pleasure.

- Say that all belongings are for your personal use, unless it's obvious that you're bringing in a gift.

- Never go through customs with illegal drugs, not even a small amount of marijuana. Do not carry more than a quart of liquor or a carton of cigarettes.

- Remove all film from its boxes to show that you have no intention of reselling it. You can usually avoid paying duties on large quantities of film for your personal use in this way.

Getting foreign currency

- Note: the rate of exchange is usually poor at airports and other locations where travelers are most dependent on the service.

- Exchange only enough to cover costs from the airport to your hotel (usually $20.00 is enough).

LUGGAGE HANDLING

Your luggage presents you with many possibilities for trouble. Of course, the lighter you travel, the less the likelihood will be for snags—but here are a few helpful ideas to avoid them.

Getting a porter

Once you're through customs you can hire a porter (though porters are a vanishing breed). Most travelers nowadays can get by without them, though.

- In order to assure a fair price, ask the charge per bag before the porter picks any of them up.

- If you're handicapped or have any serious medical problems, ask the airline for help in getting from the airplane, through customs, and on your way to your hotel.

Losing luggage

It's frustrating to lose luggage. If you've followed the advice of never packing irreplaceable items in bags you check on to the plane, however, you'll be relatively calm in your dealings with the airline. And that's the best way to be.

- Report the loss immediately to the airline representative. Be polite but vocal about the loss and note the representative's name.

- If the airline can't find your bags after checking the plane and baggage area, file a written claim notice immediately. Give a detailed list of the contents of the lost luggage.

- Make sure you get a copy of the claim and do not surrender your claim checks, the only proof you have that the airline has indeed lost your bags. If the airline insists on keeping a claim check, get a written receipt for it and the name of the person who takes it from you.

Making do when your luggage is lost

- Ask the airline representative for an overnight kit and emergency funds to purchase essential clothes and toiletries. Even if the luggage is found, you can keep the kit and anything you've purchased with the money (but be fair in your demands).

- Ask the airline to deliver your bags to your hotel in town if they are recovered shortly.

- If the airline loses your luggage permanently, you'll be paid a set amount per pound by the airline, usually no more than $700. The exact reimbursement plan is on your ticket.

- You'll be paid more than that if you've taken out extra luggage insurance (see p. 19).

Dealing with damaged luggage

- If there is any sign of damage to your bag, check the contents immediately.

- If you find damaged goods, file a claim immediately with an airline representative. Make sure you get a copy of the claim form. You'll be reimbursed for damage done to the bag or its contents.

- **Any** bag which is overpacked will disqualify a claim.

GETTING FROM AIRPORTS TO HOTELS

You'll almost always find relatively inexpensive local transportation to take you from an airport into the center of a town or city.

Finding cheap transportation

- Go to the airline counter, the information booth, or the local tourist office and simply ask for the most economical way to get into town.

- Several people can sometimes split the cost of a taxi and come out ahead. But most of the time local buses will offer the best value.

- If you want to take a taxi, ask the airline or information clerk for the approximate cost of the trip and about tipping practices and percentages.

- When you enter the bus or taxi, show the driver the name and address of your hotel and be sure he can take you to your destination.

10

HOTEL STRATEGIES

In this chapter you'll find helpful tips on everything from getting settled in a hotel to stays in boardinghouses and youth hostels. The information may help make your stay in Europe an experience truly worth remembering.

ARRIVING AT A HOTEL

Getting settled in a hotel may or may not take long. Many things can go awry. Here's how to avoid problems.

Bringing bags into a hotel

Whether you use public transportation or a taxi, you'll eventually arrive at the steps of your hotel. Taxi drivers normally do little more than remove the bags from the car and set them on the curb.

- If the driver carries your bags into the hotel, you should tip him as you would a hotel porter. Normally, whoever is behind the desk will see you struggling and come to your aid, if the cabby doesn't.

- Do not leave bags unattended on the curb while you search for someone to bring them into the hotel.

Checking into a hotel

At the front desk, give the clerk your name and the dates of your reservations. You will then be asked to fill out a police form. If you've memorized the number, date, and place of issue of your passport, filling out this form will be easy.

- If the clerk asks for your passport so that he can fill out the form for you, tell him you'd rather do it yourself.

- If he insists, give him half an hour to return it (a little longer in Portugal, where the local police may need to see it). Under no circumstances should you surrender it for longer—it's your document, and you need it!

- While you're checking in, ask the clerk for stationery or matches—something with the hotel's name and address on it. It may sound ridiculous, but almost everyone forgets the name and address of one of their hotels at some time during a trip!

Hotel costs and services

Check-in is the time to get everything straight on costs and services. Avoid conflicts by asking questions right away.

- Is the cost of breakfast, or any other meal, included with the room price?
- Will there be any additional service charges?
- What's the tax on rooms and services?
- Are there any additional charges for laundry, local calls, television, etc.?
- How much does a bath cost?
- Does the hotel supply towels with the bath?

Checking your room out

If the porter shows you to your room, tip according to the amount of luggage. If there's anything wrong or you want to change rooms, let the desk clerk know right now!

- Check the room for noise. A room near a subway or railroad, overlooking a main boulevard, next to the elevator, or by a bathroom is hard to sleep in.
- Check the smell: does the room smell fresh and clean?
- Check the posted price on the wall or on the back of the door. Does it match the one quoted to you in the lobby?
- Check for hot water—it can be a luxury in a small hotel. Do the faucets drip?
- Check the heat: if you'll need it, make sure the system is working. This can be difficult, since some hotels shut off heat during the day. Ask whether a space heater is available.
- Check the bath room (or shower) and the WC. Many superb small hotels don't have baths or showers in individual rooms—accept this and the subsequent savings!
- Check the bedding. If you must have an American-style pillow, make sure one is available (they're often stuffed in closets or bureaus). Ask about extra blankets if you'll need them.

Getting bumped despite written confirmation

Many hotels overbook by 10 to 15 percent to make up for no-shows and then bump the overflow. Unfortunately, if you don't have a **written** confirmation of reservations, you have no legitimate grounds for complaints. But if you do have such confirmation, here's what to do if you're bumped.

- Insist that the hotel come up with a room. Also insist

that they pay your cab fare from the hotel to a new hotel if you must move.

- If the management refuses to do anything, create a small scene. No hotel likes a scene in its front lobby! The very least the hotel should do is to pay your way to the local room-finding service (see below).

Getting bumped without written confirmation

Unless you have a written confirmation, you can expect no sympathy. A telephone conversation or a voucher may be helpful, but neither is enough. That's why you should insist on written confirmations.

- Stay calm and polite. Ask the clerk to help you to find a room. He or she will often make many phone calls to help a stranded tourist.

- Failing that, get directions to a room-finding service (see below).

RESERVATION SERVICES

The big advantage of traveling without reservations is the overall freedom it gives you. Many people prefer to travel in this fashion. When you arrive in a city without a room reserved, you can almost always get one from a reservation service.

Tourist information offices

When you arrive in a strange city without a room reservation, go directly to the nearest tourist information office. These are located in railway stations, airports, docks, and in the center of cities and smaller towns. If you don't know where the tourist office is, the clerk at the nearest hotel can tell you.

- Many of these offices have a room-finding service or can direct you to one. They are generally open from 9:00 or 10:00 a.m. to 10:00 or 11:00 p.m., though they may close on holidays and Sundays.

- You're always served on a first-come, first-served basis. Time will pass more quickly if you bring a snack and something to read while you wait.

- When you're served, tell the clerk what price range you want. Note that the cheapest rooms fill up fast in peak seasons and may not be available. It will take anywhere from ten minutes to two hours to book a room.

- Ask about the fee structure for booking and determine how much it will cost before you book a room.

- When a room is found and booked, ask the clerk to

mark its location on a free map that the tourist office will have. Write down its full name and address as well—partial information or unknown locations spell trouble.

- For members of racial minorities: discrimination is virtually impossible when you use room-booking services.

Other booking services

- **American Express** offers a room-finding service on a fee-paid basis. So do many other large travel agencies. However, most of these deal in higher-priced rooms.

- **Airline offices** often have books listing good, moderate-to-expensive hotels. If you have a ticket through an airline, you can often get room-finding information and help.

- **Student offices** can locate rooms for those who qualify either by age or student status. You can get lists of foreign student offices from the CIEE (see p. 16).

- **YWCA/YMCAs** and **youth hostel organizations** can also be of help (see pp. 108-109).

FINDING YOUR OWN ROOM

The alternative to having an agent or a tourist office clerk book a room for you is obvious—book one yourself! The big advantage of this approach over the others is that you get to see the room (and the hotel) before you rent. That advantage pales in extremely crowded cities during the peak season, but the fact is that you often do better on your own than when others book for you. It's quite easy and can save you a bundle if you know a few basic principles and techniques.

Hotel rates

- In general, the larger the hotel, the higher the rates. "Name-brand" hotels are especially expensive.

- Almost all hotels in Europe have a wide variety of rooms that vary from abysmal to great. Even in large and overly expensive hotels, you may find a bargain.

- The more Americans in a hotel, the higher the rates. Americans are just not bargain-hunters when it comes to lodgings. The British, Scandinavians, and Germans tend to be more skillful travelers—watch for them in smaller hotels offering more for your money.

- Hotels grow progressively more expensive as they get close to the heart of the city. Near the airport, railway station, or dock of main cities, you'll also find inflated rates.

- During festivals, pilgrimages, sporting events, fairs, and conventions, all rooms are overpriced—if you can find any at all—even on the outskirts of town.

Hotels in outlying areas

On the fringes of larger cities, you'll find the kind of small hotels that make a trip to Europe memorable. True, you will have to commute to city centers for sightseeing, but it will be worth your while to check out these hotels for several reasons.

- Hotel rates in outlying areas are low!

- These hotels are not what every American has seen or visited, and are more typical of the area you are in.

- You may have to forego television or a private bath, but you'll meet Europeans more readily.

- Many hotels in outlying areas are far from bright lights and traffic, so you'll sleep better there.

Using a travel guide to find lodging

- Use the guides listed on p. 22 to help you find lodging. Travel guides are most useful for the off-season, from late September through April.

- Buy a guide that lists telephone numbers along with the hotel descriptions.

- If you want to avoid the expense of making many calls, go to an area that's thick with listings. Then check that area out on foot. Often this will lead you to a gem that's not even listed.

- To get a room in a crowded city, your timing must be right: the earlier you try, the better the odds are.

Room-hunting preliminaries

- Never judge a hotel by its exterior or lobby. Smaller, less expensive hotels may not put money into appearances but may still offer comfortable, charming, clean accommodations.

- Go into the hotel and ask the person at the front desk if a room is available. (See p. 100 for ways to get past a "No Vacancy" sign.) Ask for room rates. If one's open in your range, ask to see it. If none are open, ask whether a nearby hotel has rooms and rates that suit you.

- If there's a room open in your price range, look at it

before renting it (see p. 95). Then you can begin to
bargain.

Bargaining on room rates

Once you find a room you like, you'll want to come up with the
best price possible. Although it goes against the American grain,
bargaining in various ways is acceptable throughout much of Europe.
Naturally, it's only effective in an area with many open rooms, and for
that reason it's done more successfully in the off season.

- Remember that you can play a big part in determining
  the price of the room.

- Begin by being flexible. Tell the clerk that the room is
  great, but that it's too expensive for you. This will often
  bring the price down.

- Or be blunt: tell the clerk that you like the room and will
  pay such and such an amount—a lower, but still fair,
  price. This also works frequently, but you have to have
  the right temperament to try it.

- Or be hesitant: a clerk can sense this. He'll often respond by showing you a room that's just as nice but
  costs less.

- If you find a hotel you like in which the cheaper rooms
  are filled, ask whether you can rent a more expensive
  room for one night and then move to a cheaper one the
  next day. This puts the clerk in the position of weighing
  a cost reduction against the bother and cost of cleaning an extra set of sheets. Sometimes a clerk will agree
  to give you the more expensive room at a lower rate to
  avoid moving you at all.

Room-rate discounts

- You should get a room-rate discount in most countries
  during the off season. Rates posted in a room vary from
  a minimum (off-season) to a maximum (peak season).
  Insist upon the lower rate in the off season!

- You should not have to pay as much for a double bed as
  for two twins in comparable rooms, since the hotel
  saves money on the number of sheets it has to wash.

- Always ask about discounts for prolonged stays (usually three days or longer). If none exist, the hotel will tell
  you so. You can then either accept the standard rate or
  shop around.

- Ask if the hotel offers weekend discounts, especially at
  hotels in larger cities appealing to business people.

- Try to rent a room without breakfast included, since

continental breakfasts will cost you several dollars. During the peak season many hotels refuse to do this, but in the off season most of them give in.

Beating the "No Vacancy" sign

It can be frustrating at times, this process of finding a room on your own. It's particularly frustrating when you see **No Vacancy** on every door (**Complet, Besetz, Occupato**—dirty words when you're looking for a room). When things look very bleak, try some of the following techniques to help you come up with a room.

- Tell the clerk that you stayed in this hotel once before and want very badly to stay here again. When he tries to remember your face, tell him how much you liked the hotel and the town. He may sense that you're lying; if he's got a good memory, he'll be sure of it. But he'll smile, try to find you a room in the hotel, or call one of his friends in a hotel down the street.

- When you walk up to the clerk and the first thing you hear is, "How long do you intend to stay?" you've got to answer, "A week," or there may suddenly be no vacancies. Short stays cost hotels more in overhead.

- At about 11:00 p.m., walk into the lobby of a small hotel, hand the clerk a piece of paper with the hotel's name scribbled on it, tell the clerk that André Papillon (make up any name) recommended the place to you, and ask him if there might be a room available. At this point the clerk may take the gamble of giving you a room reserved for someone else. The hotel collects double, and you have a room.

- In desperation, try a taxi driver. The word **hotel** is an international one. The driver may just steer you to a nearby spot. More than likely he'll take you for a ride, but the ride as a bribe sometimes pays off.

Miscellaneous charges

Watch for miscellaneous charges. Unless you understand them in advance, you'll end up paying far more than you planned on.

- Prices for hotel rooms are sometimes quoted on a **per person** basis, especially in Italy and Spain. Get the price straight to start with: "Is that per person or the total price of the room?"

- Avoid having the hotel set up tours or arrange for nights on the town. Naturally, this is a legitimate part of their business, but you'll save money if you only use them when you really can't get tickets or tour seats yourself.

- If you make long distance phone calls from a hotel room, you can legally be socked with a surcharge that may be as much as 40 percent on any bill. Therefore, before making such calls, find out about possible surcharges. If they seem steep, make your call from the central post office.

- If there's a charge for hotel parking, just leave your car in the street under a light. Be sure to remove all your belongings from the car and lock it.

Room and board

The term **full room and board (pension complet)** means that you're staying in a hotel and eating all meals there. **Half room and board (demi pension)** indicates that you're skipping either lunch or dinner at the hotel. Most European hotels offer good rates for both full and half room and board arrangements.

- If you're eating meals at your hotel, see whether there is a discount for full or half room and board. Make sure any discounts you opt for show up on your final bill.

- Some hotels will even force you to have meals there before they will rent you a room. In the peak season you may have to submit to this racket, intended to jack up the price of government-controlled room rates.

- Many hotels will not offer room and board discounts unless you stay for a minimum of three days. But they won't tell you this in advance, so ask about it.

- If you do stay on a room-and-board basis, find out whether there is an extra charge for anything, such as wine, dessert, or coffee.

- As unbelievable as it may sound, you must pay an extra charge in some hotels for **not** eating breakfast. You may as well eat if you're being charged for it!

- In resort areas, many luxury hotels have agreements for reciprocal lunches and dinners for guests staying on room-and-board terms. Ask the clerk at the front desk for information on such arrangements.

IDIOSYNCRASIES OF EUROPEAN HOTELS

Half the pleasure of travel comes from discovering the difference between them and us. However, some differences come as a shock. Here are some bridges for cultural gaps in hotels.

The front desk

- Get the clerk's name when you check in. Ask for all prices to be written down on a slip of paper to avoid confusion about rates at check-out time.

- Don't assume that your name is easy to spell or read. Write it down for the clerk.

- Ask as late in the day as possible for a morning wake-up call. With luck you'll be leaving it with the person responsible for calling you in the morning, and your message won't go astray.

Elevators

- The elevators in most hotels do not work like Swiss watches. The clunk when you push the call button means it's heard you. The whine means it's on its way. The second clunk means the maid has intercepted it on the third floor and will now head in the opposite direction.

- Once you've cornered the elevator, you must shut the outer gate tightly before closing the inner door and pushing the floor button. If the gate isn't closed, the elevator won't work—no matter how much you swear.

Bath rooms and showers

Although the trend in Europe is toward the American-style hotel room that includes a tub or shower, many European hotels have detached rooms for bathing.

The room with the shower or bath is always separate from the toilet (WC). Both may be at the end of the hall, but they could also be four floors up, tucked under the slanted roof where only cats and bats can live.

You often have to get a key for the bath or shower room from the clerk at the front desk. The clerk will ask the maid to bring you a towel.

- Ask the owner about the best time to take a bath. Some hotels arrange hours for their guests so as not to disturb sleep.

- You pay extra per shower or bath unless you've agreed that it's included in the price of the room.

- There are public baths in most cities. You'll also find them in many train stations.

Hot and cold water

- In small hotels with a central water heating system you may be out of luck (and hot water) if you don't time your bath or shower properly.

- The red spot on a faucet means hot, the blue means cold. After five minutes of running the red spot without getting warm water, assume the plumber was blind or, more likely, the hotel is out of hot water.

- Quite a few hotels have individual gas water-heater units for the shower or bath. When you turn on the hot water faucet, the unit will burst into flame, heating only the water you'll need.

- The water will be scalding. The trick for getting the right temperature is to turn the hot water on full and turn the cold water on—gently, or you'll end up with a cold stream shooting at you. The code of the road in the bath room is that cold water has priority over hot.

- One out of ten small European hotels has broken pipes.

Toilets

- Toilets are generally labelled "WC" (water closet) and are intended for both sexes if they're not otherwise designated (Watch out for "**signori**" and "**signore**," for men and women respectively, in Italy).

- Many toilets do not have a light switch. As soon as you lock the door, the light will go on.

- If the light doesn't go on, the switch may be on the outside of the toilet.

- Light a match or two in smelly toilets. You won't notice the smell.

- Most toilets have some form of toilet paper: real stuff, slices of newspaper, a kind of dark crepe paper, magazine pages. Some don't have any—a good reason to carry some tissue in your purse or wallet.

- In some parts of Europe, toilets are no more than holes in the floor with two tile steps to squat on. You feel like an experienced traveler after you've visited your first **steppe!**

Bidets

You'll find bidets in many European hotel rooms and WCs. If you care to experiment with these toilet-shaped porcelain fixtures for your personal hygiene, do so (Europeans can't believe that Americans do without them in their bathrooms!).

- Otherwise, use them for sponge baths, for hair washing, or for hand washing clothes.

Mattresses and bedding

- If you're the kind of person who doesn't have to jump to sink a basket, ask to see the bed in a room before renting it. You may have to settle for a double bed on which you can lie diagonally.

- You'll run into a mattress every now and then which gives you a spinal tap for no extra charge. Just toss it on the floor and sleep there.

- In some countries, you'll find pillows which look like short, rolled-up rugs. If you don't like them, check in the closet or bureau drawers for American-style pillows (**oreillers**). If you can't find any, ask the front desk for some. If they don't have any, you're stuck.

- Many European hotels substitute wedge-shaped bolsters under the mattress for pillows. If you don't like these, just pull them out and look or ask for American-style pillows.

- Pat the feathers in the down quilts you'll find in Germany, Austria, Italy, and Scandinavia until they spread out evenly under the thick white cover. Then toss the comforter up and down a few times. This fluffs up the feathers. You place the whole thing over you, covering most of your body.

- If you want to slide two beds together to make one, place the box springs side by side, but always place the mattresses **across** them. If you don't, someone will disappear in the night.

Lights

The lights in the hall can be a problem in some hotels, since they'll only stay on for a minute after you push a button on the wall. This conserves electricity but forces you to grope for that button if you don't want to trip and fall down the stairs.

- You may want to carry a small flashlight and beat the system.

- Turn off the lights in your room when you leave, or Frau Weber, with characteristic wit, will say, "So you think this is Christmas?"

- If you want strong lights for reading, you may have to carry a high-wattage bulb with you.

Guests

Hotels are strict about inviting guests to your room. The landlady will look at you and your new friend heading up the stairs and say, "Excuse me. You paid for one person, not two."

- If you are expecting, or hope to find, a partner, pay for two from the start.

- In most countries it is illegal for unmarried people to

share a room. The restriction is almost universally ignored as long as the bill has been properly paid.

Maids

The maid will do everything possible to wake you up. If your door isn't locked, she'll open it, say the equivalent of "oops!", then slam it closed. You can avoid this by locking the door when you go to bed and placing a "Do Not Disturb" sign (if there is one) on the outside knob. Some experienced travelers carry such a sign with them for hotels poorly supplied with such vital amenities. But this won't stop the maid from jabbering with other maids in the hall, coughing, laughing, singing, telling jokes, and making other cleaning maid sounds—which are not very subtle ways of letting you know that it's time for her to make your bed.

- Unless you put small things in a drawer or in your luggage, they may disappear. They're usually not being stolen, but are being thrown away.

LAUNDRY

You'll see placards in every hotel telling you that it's illegal to wash clothes in your room; virtually every traveler ignores this warning. By hand washing your clothes you'll save money and time (hotel laundries take three days!). Besides, today's modern fabrics are practically maintenance-free.

Washing clothes in your room

- Roll clothes in a towel to collect excess moisture and speed up drying before you hang them up. (But don't wring out drip-dry clothes.)
- Be sure to bring a braided rubber clothesline from which you can hang wash to dry.

Hanging clothes to dry

- Never hang your laundry out a window to dry. That will cause an international incident, either with the maid or with the management itself.
- Don't lay wet clothes on a stained wood surface, since they'll bleach the wood and end up stained themselves.
- Separate the back portion of any wet clothing from the front.
- Smooth out the material to eliminate potential wrinkles.
- Button the top two buttons of a shirt and set the collar in the correct position.

Wrinkles, lint, and stains

- To get rid of wrinkles in shirts, skirts, slacks, or dresses after they are dry, hang them in a steamy bathroom.

- Use any kind of tape to pick up lint off clothes.

- Soak blood stains in cold water to remove them.

- Sprinkle salt or soda on wine stains and talcum powder on grease stains to help absorb and remove them before washing.

11
ALTERNATIVES TO HOTELS

There is a wide variety of accommodations available in Europe. If you're on a budget or if you prefer a more intimate experience than hotels can offer, boardinghouses, youth hostels and other youth-oriented accommodations, and camping (or simply sleeping out) will give you plenty of options to consider.

BOARDINGHOUSES

Boardinghouses (**pensions**) are as common in Europe as hotels. They offer most of the advantages of hotels and the added element of personal attention. They provide rooms and meals at reasonable prices.

The rate in a pension varies according to the room-and-board plan being offered. The full pension (**pension complet**) arrangement includes all meals plus a room, while half pension (**demi pension**) covers the room, breakfast, and either lunch or supper.

Boardinghouse rates

- Note that the basic room rate generally includes the cost of breakfast and the price of a bath; but you'll have to work this out in advance.

- Have the price of the room written down on a slip of paper and hang on to it. Or pay ahead of time. This way any misunderstandings, hidden service charges, and surprise taxes will surface before you move in.

- If you plan to stay in a boardinghouse for more than three days, ask about long-term rates. The difference may really surprise you.

Food at boardinghouses

Meals are generally served at a common table where you'll get to know the other boarders.

- You are not expected to tip the cook or maid, although a token tip would be in order when you leave.

- If you want to affect the quality of the cooking, tell the cook honestly what you think of different dishes, either verbally or in sign language.

- Never start off with a full pension (**pension complet**) agreement. You want to be able to eat out at local restaurants as well. If a boardinghouse insists that you eat all meals there, look somewhere else for a room.

YOUTH HOSTELS AND YOUTH ACCOMMODATIONS

There is a network of over two thousand hostels in Europe, including camps, castles, lodges, huts, villas, ships, and schools. They're interesting because the people who stay in them are real adventurers.

The American Youth Hostels (AYH) association issues youth hostel cards, which you must have if you're planning to hostel your way around Europe. Costs vary according to your age. You can get information from any local branch or the central office: American Youth Hostels, Delaplane, VA 22025.

Technically, as an American, you can't get a youth hostel card abroad, but many Americans get around this by giving a foreign address.

Basics of hostels

- Check ahead if you're about 25 or older, since some hostels impose age limits to keep room available for youths.

- Bring a sleeping sack (like a sheet), which you can make yourself or pick up from the Metropolitan New York Council, 132 Spring Street, New York, NY 10012. Some hostels insist that you have such a sheet, while others provide them or let the rules slide. Sleeping arrangements are mostly dormitory-style set-ups on simple cots.

- Save money by trying out the communal dining rooms. The meals are filling and sometimes quite good.

- When you find that a certain hostel restricts its space to foot travelers, park your car around the corner and hike in.

Ground rules for hostels

- You help with the cleaning.

- Neither smoking nor radios are permitted in the sleeping area.

- No alcohol is allowed except with meals in France, Italy, Portugal, and Spain.

- There's a three-day limit on stays (unless there's lots of room).

- Lights go out by 10:00 p.m., and you get up by 7:00 a.m.

- Hostels often close from late morning to late afternoon—so get there early to register for the coming night!

- Many hostels will take reservations for the next day. All it costs is the price of a phone call.

- If you want to reserve a room in advance, write to the hostel requesting a reservation. Enclose one night's fee and enough international reply coupons to cover an airmail reply.

Inexpensive, youth-oriented rooms

- If you're young and on a budget, take advantage of the many youth-oriented facilities available, which include student hotels, dormitories, and the many YMCA/YWCAs throughout Europe.

- Get information on the latter as far in advance as possible, making reservations by mail in time to beat the summer rush!

- For information on facilities abroad, contact the YMCA, 291 Broadway, New York, NY 10007, (212) 374-2000; YWCA, 600 Lexington Avenue, New York, NY 10022, (212) 753-4700; or any branch of these organizations in your local area.

- For information on student hotels and dormitories, contact the CIEE (see p. 16).

- Note that facilities in Europe tend to be better than those in the U.S.

- Note too that you will find better facilities in central and northern Europe than in the south.

CAMPING

Camping is geared to a loose, free-flowing style of travel that is not compatible with limited time. If you've got the time, however, you'll find that European campgrounds are well organized, often offering facilities that include showers and grocery stores. You'll find them everywhere, even in major European cities.

International camping carnet

- Get an International Camping Carnet, the passport to camping abroad, which entitles you to small reductions in fees. Contact National Campers and Hikers Association, 7172 Transit Road, Buffalo, NY 14221, or AAA, 8111 Gatehouse Road, Falls Church, VA 22047.

- If you forget to pick one up in the U.S., ask for one at an automobile association abroad.

Camping equipment

- Know your outfit before traveling abroad, which means trying it out in the U.S. before you leave. Nothing's worse than a so-called waterproof tent which lets the rain in or a mosquito net that's worn through. If you camp out before going to Europe, you'll find out quickly what gear you're missing (or what miserable gear you've got).

- Bring the minimum gear: sleeping bag (down, or comparable synthetic), plastic sheet, tent, warm clothes, bug spray, and flask.

- Bring a good knife with a corkscrew and bottle opener. A Swiss Army knife is excellent.

- Plan to use a butane stove and a large, refillable cylinder of gas. Buy these abroad.

- Travel by car, not by truck or trailer. Can you imagine taking a trip to a fjord in a car pulling a trailer?

Camping etiquette

- Always ask permission to camp out on someone's property.

- Avoid using fires; they are illegal in almost all areas.

- Leave the campsite spotless.

- Note that in Europe, saying thank you and goodbye to your host, with a handshake, is **minimal** good manners.

SLEEPING OUT AND OTHER TACTICS

Thousands of young people travel throughout Europe each year without spending a cent for a hotel room. While this practice is officially discouraged by most police departments, it's nevertheless tolerated in most countries. Be cautious in eastern Europe, though.

Sleeping out

Sleeping out is a cinch in most rural areas. It has some advantages over sleeping in campgrounds, where you have to pay an entrance fee for the privilege of being surrounded by a milling crowd. You'll become a part of the spot you've chosen: the farmer waking you up could either ask you to leave or invite you to have breakfast with him!

- Try to find as isolated and protected a spot as possible.

- Be prepared to end up with two cat's eyes peering down at you over a flashlight in the middle of the night. Be polite, show your visitor your passport, offer him or her a cigarette.

- Consider paying the small entrance fee for a campground when you are in a city. It's harder to sleep out in urban areas.

Alternatives to sleeping out

- Try the train station: it's the warmest, safest place to sleep for free in cities. The police will wake you up if you're lying down; but if you can sleep sitting up, you've got it made.

- Don't count on getting the police to put you up in a cell for the night if you can't find a room in a crowded town. Usually, the police will not want you around, since many unpleasant things can happen in jails.

- If you have a Eurailpass, try sleeping on trains. This is less comfortable than some know-it-all travel writers insist (they've never done it). If you try it, be sure to pull out the leg support (if there is one) from underneath your seat.

- For men only: if you have friends in the army, try to stay with them in the barracks. Although this is quite illegal, it will save you a wad. Someone always pulls night duty, which will leave a bunk open for you.

Rooms for free

If you get along well with a European, it's possible that you'll be invited to stay in his or her home. Bring a small token gift (a bouquet, American stamps or books, Kennedy coins) when you arrive. And remember the saying, "Fish and visitors stink after three days."

You can also use a number of organizations to arrange such stays.

- SERVAS (worldwide), U.S. SERVAS Committee, Inc., Box 790, Old Chelsea Station, P.O. New York, NY 10011.

- International Hospitality Service (worldwide), International Hospitality Service, Suite 3, 1377 9th Ave, San Francisco, CA 94122.

- People-to-People (Scandinavia), U.S. Traveller's Club, P.O. Box A147, Berkeley, CA 94709.

- Club des 4 Vents (France), Club des 4 Vents, 1 rue Gozin, Paris 5ê, France.

- Centre Régionale des Oeuvres, Universitaires, Service du Logement (France), CROUS, 15 rue Soufflot, Paris 5ê, France.

- Alliance Française (France), Alliance Française, 101 Boulevard Raspail, Paris 5ê, France.

12

MONEY MATTERS AND SAFETY

FOREIGN CURRENCY

One of the realities of foreign travel is the necessity to exchange American money for foreign currency. You'll need your passport for each exchange. Money-changers charge a fee for their service. **Each time you exchange money, you lose money.** The more exchanges, the greater the loss.

Rates of exchange are posted at banks, in American Express and other travel offices, and at money-changers' offices. Rates fluctuate daily.

Exchanging currency

- Study foreign currency and coins until you are familiar with all the denominations you'll be dealing with. Just as in the U.S., size and value may not be related—small coins may be worth more than larger ones.

- If the foreign country's monetary system is not clear to you, have someone explain it. This will save you money in the long run!

- Find out the banking hours and dates of bank holidays of the place you're visiting.

- Don't make fun of foreign currency in public, even if some of the coins will float on water or the paper money would pass as newspaper.

- Never ask how much a foreign currency is worth in **real** money. It's just as real as American currency.

Getting the best deal on currency exchanges

- Never buy foreign currency in the States: you'll get only 80 percent of its real value.

- Exchange only about $20 when first arriving abroad—enough to get you to your hotel.

- Avoid exchanging money in airports, train stations, and hotels. Wherever exchange is most convenient, it's most costly.

- Never exchange money at the border between two countries, for the same reason.

- Know the current rate of exchange before you go shopping. Some shops **always** give a better rate of exchange than banks as a way of encouraging shoppers to return (a kind of built-in discount). Others try to rip you off.

Where to exchange money daily

- Exchange your money daily in reputable banks or in traveler's check offices.

- Exchange traveler's checks at their own name-brand offices in order to get the most favorable rates.

- Don't deal with money-changers. Although their rates vary from favorable to unfavorable, they offer a less favorable rate of exchange overall.

- If saving money is more important to you than saving time, check several banks before you exchange currency. Rates sometimes vary from one bank to another, and the right choice can save you 2 to 4 percent.

How much to exchange

- Most banks and traveler's check companies charge a set service fee per transaction. Thus the person who exchanges small amounts frequently gets burned. **The minimum anyone should exchange on a routine basis is the most he or she can afford to lose.**

- You'll sometimes get better rates of exchange for larger amounts, usually over one hundred dollars.

- Never carry coins across a border, since most banks won't exchange them. Either use them up or convert them to paper bills. Of course, if you intend to return to a country, some loose change won't hurt!

TRAVELER'S CHECKS

Everyone knows that it's foolish to travel abroad carrying only cash. If you carry traveler's checks, there are only two possible problems: you can't get someone to accept them, or you lose them. Fortunately, there are solutions to both problems.

Getting traveler's checks accepted

You'll sometimes run into a place that won't take your traveler's check. If this happens, you can try two things before going elsewhere.

- Ask the person in charge to call the nearest bank. Try not to create a scene, but be polite and firm in your suggestion that he or she verify the authenticity of such checks.

- Volunteer to go over to the bank and cash your check there.

Lost traveler's checks

Keep a record of your checks—both cashed and uncashed—separate from the checks themselves. For example, don't carry them both in your wallet. If you should lose your checks, do the following things.

- Go to the branch office of the company that issued the checks and report the loss there.

- Be sure to bring your passport as identification.

- Note that Avis will refund up to $100 in lost American Express checks on weekends and holidays if American Express offices are closed.

CREDIT CARDS AND MONEY

Many travelers enjoy the convenience of credit cards while they're in Europe. If you use yours, be careful to protect them.

Protecting credit cards

- Take along only the credit cards you'll need; leave all others at home in a safe deposit box. Protect credit cards as you would cash or your passport.

- Keep a list of all the numbers on cards you take in case you lose them. Take the list with you to Europe and leave a duplicate list with a friend at home.

- Note how many cards you're carrying and count them periodically. Many thieves are smart enough to take only one or two cards from a wallet, making the theft less noticeable.

- When you charge something, be sure to verify the total amount charged to you, sign the charge slip, and keep the customer copy. Unfortunately, a growing number of establishments alter charge slips in an effort to defraud customers. An extra digit on the charge slip can cause the bill to soar by a hundred dollars or more. Never throw your slips away until the charges have been billed and paid!

- Ask shops, restaurants, and hotels to convert total amounts into dollars and cents and then write the amount on the charge slip. This way you know exactly what you'll owe your credit card company despite currency fluctuations!

Using credit cards to get cash

- With an American Express card, you can get $50 in cash and $450 in traveler's checks for a 1 percent fee with a personal check.

- No personal check? They'll give you a blank one with a $50 limit.

- With a Visa card, the limit is $150.

- With Diners Club International (Amoco), you can cash checks at participating hotel chains: Holiday Inns, Howard Johnson's, Ramada Inns, and Sheridan Hotels.

- You'll always need both the credit card and your passport for these transactions.

When the money runs out

- You can wire home and ask someone to send you an international money order.

- The American Consulate can help in emergencies. But you'll have to repay money lent to you before you will be allowed to travel abroad again.

- If you haven't got enough money to pay duty on your return to the U.S., customs will take a personal check with two forms of identification.

- As ghoulish as it may sound, the easiest way to pick up a small amount of cash when you're **really** in a tight pinch is to sell a pint of your blood.

TIPPING

About the only Western European country where tips are generally frowned upon is Iceland, which makes traveling very simple there. Tipping policies are very complex in all other countries. The smartest thing you can do is to ask travel agents, airline people, and those who give you service about the tipping policy in each area.

Confusion about tipping can add 10 to 20 percent to the total cost of a trip. Here are some basics for you to follow, so that your tipping will be proper but not extravagant.

When tips are included

- Although tour packages generally include all gratuities for services included in the tour contract, ask about the policy on tipping before signing a contract.

- Ocean liner ticket prices may or may not cover tips, so

you should check into the tipping policy upon boarding.

- Airline personnel do not expect tips.

- At most European restaurants and hotels, a tip will automatically be added to your bill in the form of a service charge of 10 to 20 percent of the total bill. If you pay this charge, you're not expected to add an additional tip.

Separate tips

- You should always tip a maitre d', waiter, wine steward, porter, doorman, bellman, chambermaid, bartender, concierge, or service person for any unusual or extraordinarily fine service.

- You should tip cab drivers, provided that a service charge has not been included in the fare on the meter. Service charges are often included on meters in Belgium, Denmark, and the Netherlands. Ask if you're not sure.

- You should tip washroom attendants if you use their services. Give them as little as you can get away with.

- You should tip theater (and movie) ushers who guide you to your seat—again, a very small amount will do.

PROTECTING YOURSELF AND YOUR BELONGINGS

Suspicion and wariness require energy and are not very pleasant sensations, but they do prevent trouble, which would be even more unpleasant.

Discouraging theft

- Never flash money or showy jewelry about. I suggest that you leave expensive jewelry at home.

- For men: place all valuables in a pouch and hang it around your neck if you don't wear a jacket. Use a long leather thong that allows the pouch to dangle just above your waist. Don't put your wallet in your hip pocket.

- For women: never put your purse in coat pockets, in shopping carts, or on counters. The only safe way to carry a purse is to hug it tightly against your side, protected by your arm.

- Don't set anything valuable near an open window or on a curbside table (as when dining al fresco).

- Don't carry cameras hanging around your neck. Thieves just pull them off—hurting your neck in the process!

- Don't hire a car with license plates from outside the country you're in, except in Italy (see p. 146).

- Never leave valuables in a car. To show that you haven't done so, leave the glove compartment open while you're away from the car.

- Note: almost all hotel rooms have doors with locks and bolt locks. Use them. If the door doesn't close tightly or if the locks seem flimsy, jam a chair underneath the knob to make it difficult to open.

Storing valuables

- Don't put valuables in a camera case. Thieves have caught on to this practice.

- When staying at a hotel, use the safe to store all your valuables each night.

- When getting valuables out of the safe, be attentive. This is one time when thieves will try to distract you.

Thwarting pickpockets

- Be wary of minor accidents: being bumped, having your foot stepped upon, being shoved. If your mind is not on your money, you will be vulnerable to pickpockets.

- If you're being pushed around in a crowd, drop your arms and turn around to face the person bumping you. A thief will tend to turn his head and move away quickly.

- Watch for drunks who try to put their arms around you. Don't let them: they may be feeling for your wallet.

- Whenever a fight breaks out, move away as quickly and as unobtrusively as possible. Avoid commotions of all kinds (pickpockets love to create them).

Preventing muggings

- During the day, walk close to walls. Do the opposite at night, walking far away from the walls.

- Never turn your back completely to the sidewalk when looking for a house number or unlocking a door.

- If you've just been to the bank and are carrying quite a bit of cash, walk against the flow of traffic. This makes it easy to spot anyone following you.

- Be wary of approaching motorbikes.

- If you go into a red light district, go sober. Most muggings occur when you're drunk. Carry the minimum amount of cash you'll need for the night in your shoes.

Handling beggars

Sometimes you have no choice but to pay off the beggar kids who crowd around you. For instance, if you leave your car to do some sightseeing, you'd do well to give the leader of the group some small coins. He then becomes your car's protector. Surprisingly, you rarely get ripped off if you pay his small fee. (Not surprisingly, if you don't pay, you may find that minor "accidents" occur in your absence.)

- Say "no" to most other requests and keep moving.

- If you are approached by a woman with a baby over her shoulder and her palm stretched out, or by a young woman asking you for money because she hasn't eaten in a week, offer her something to eat. She'll usually turn it down.

13

EATING AND DRINKING

Crusty and warm French bread fresh from the **four** ... moist filets of herring smothered in bits of onion on a piece of rich rye bread ... succulent snails simmering in sizzling garlic butter ... Spanish **paella**—chunks of chicken, meat, and seafood served on a hot bed of saffron-soaked rice ... fettucine, lasagne, rigatoni—pasta in every imaginable form ... pastries from tarts to petits fours—just a few of the taste treats that are in store for you.

There are two basic ways of ordering such food in European restaurants: **à la carte** or **table d'hôte. À la carte** means that you order and pay for each item separately. **Table d'hôte** means that you order an entire meal, from soup to nuts, for a set price.

- A set-price meal is usually a better deal than an **à la carte** meal. Most set-price meals include the cover and service charge as well as the cost of either a beer or a carafe of wine.

- Synonyms for **table d'hôte** are **tourist menu, menu, set-price meal, menu touristique, prix fixe, menu turistico, prezzo fisso.** If you want to order a set-price meal, ask the waiter to point them out to you on the menu.

FASHIONABLE RESTAURANTS

In Great Britain, better restaurants have been given star ratings by Egon Ronay (a travel writer) and the automobile clubs. These ratings are usually posted at the front entrance. On the Continent, the most reliable ratings have been done by Michelin. Once again, restaurants are proud of these ratings and display them for all to see.

Reservations

- If you absolutely must eat at a certain fine restaurant, you can make reservations from the States by writing the management and including a deposit. Better restaurants usually require reservations, although this is not a universal law.

- Or, if you are staying at a nearby hotel, ask the management there to contact the restaurant on your behalf, particularly if there's a language barrier. (This is a service that you should reward with a tip.)

- Or you can call the restaurant yourself as soon as you arrive in Europe.

Best times for best meals

Better restaurants tend to be more crowded in the evening than at lunch. So be flexible if you really want to eat in a certain place.

- If you plan to eat by yourself in a better restaurant, make reservations for an early or a very late meal. Most restaurants frown upon diners eating alone, because they take up valuable table space. By avoiding the peak hours, you'll offend no one, have better and friendlier service, and get the full attention of the kitchen.

- Prices at lunch are often considerably lower than they are in the evening, but they'll still be high. You should expect to pay twenty-five dollars or more per person in a truly fine and fashionable restaurant at noon. In the evening, the bill will run forty dollars or more per person, on an average.

Dress requirements

- Ask whether there are any dress requirements when making reservations, to avoid being turned away at the door. Very few restaurants have stringent dress codes these days.

- A dark sports coat with tie for a man and comparable dress for a woman is suitable in almost all restaurants at noon and night. However, some places insist on more formal evening attire on certain nights.

Drinking with meals

In Europe, it's considered gauche to have an American-style cocktail before dinner. Alcohol dulls taste buds and makes it more difficult to appreciate good food.

- Replace cocktails with a glass of sherry, white port, or similar light apéritif.

- Order water after ordering wine, or skip water altogether if it's not important to you. In more sophisticated restaurants, it's considered gauche to order water with your meal.

- Don't feel that you have to splurge on a high-priced wine, which will double the price of your meal. Do what most sensible and experienced gourmets advise: settle for a good, medium-priced wine that goes well with the meal.

- Order wine by the glass if you prefer, just as you would in less fancy places. This is highly recommended for people who drink lightly.

Ordering wine

- If you know which wine you want, order it.

- If the wine list does not give enough information to let you make an intelligent choice, ask the waiter or wine steward to bring several possible choices to the table. Don't hesitate to ask a wine steward or waiter for advice.

- You should be shown the bottle before it's opened. If a bottle arrives already opened, then send it back. No European would allow such a thing to pass.

- If the waiter tells you that he doesn't have the bottle of wine you ordered, but does have one just like it, ask the price. This will avoid angry confrontations at bill time.

Wine etiquette

- If you choose a red wine, ask the waiter to open it immediately to let it breathe. If it's the only wine you'll be having with your meal, you can ask him to pour it right away.

- If you choose a white wine or some Portuguese wines, note that they should be chilled. The long-necked bottles of German and Alsatian white wines make this difficult, unless they're turned upside down in an ice bucket. A good waiter will do this without being told. Don't let the wine get too cold, or it will lose some of its taste and bouquet.

- After the waiter opens a bottle, he should hand you the cork. Squeeze the cork to make sure it's solid, then give it a quick sniff to check for any rancid odor. Set it on the table. The waiter will then pour some of the wine into your glass.

- Watch out for two things as you taste it: a foul taste from the cork or an acid (vinegar) bite. You will eventually get a bad bottle of wine, and it is not bad manners to send it back. However, bad bottles are very rare.

- If you think the wine is borderline, let someone else taste it for a final decision—even the waiter. This may not be perfect etiquette, but your enjoyment should come first.

- Large wine glasses and water goblets are best for drinking wine. If you think the glasses are too small, ask for larger ones.

Wines for a Splurge

Red Wines

COUNTRY	REGION	BEST LABELS
France	Bordeaux (five-year-old)	Lafite Latour Haut-Brion
	Burgundy (three-year-old)	Romanée-Conti Le Musigny Le Chambertin Clos de Fêves Le Corton
	Beaujolais (one- to three-year-old)	Brouilly Chénas Chiroubles Côte de Brouilly Fleurie Juliénas Morgon Moulin-à-Vent Saint-Amour
	Rhône	Châteauneuf-du-Pape Côte Pôtie Hermitage
Italy	Chianti (Classico) Bardolino Barolo Valpolicella Barbaresco Gattinara (Monsecco)	
Spain	Rioja	

White Wines

COUNTRY	REGION	BEST LABELS
France	Bordeaux	Sauternes Graves
	Burgundy	Chablis Pouilly-Fuissé Saint-Véran Pinot-Chardonnay Mâcon
Germany	Mosels* Rheins	
Italy	Soave Verdicchio Orvieto	

* Look at label: **Qualitätswein** is good; **Qualitätswein mit Prädikat**, better.

European Table Manners

- It's not unusual for lunch or dinner to last two or three hours.

- You can put your forearms (not your elbows) on the table and fit right in.

- When you eat with a European, always wish him "good appetite." If you can't say it in the native language, say it in English.

- In many countries, foods will not be served simultaneously or on the same plate, but as a succession of dishes.

- Europeans eat with their forks in their left hands so that they don't have to shift them back and forth when they use their knives. (It makes sense.)

- Many restaurants use the same knife and fork for all courses. You're expected to wipe them off with a piece of your bread.

- You can also use bread to wipe the plate clean. Or put bread on a fork to mop up sauces.

- Europeans often skin fruit with a knife and fork.

- An American will spit seeds and pits into an open hand before placing them on a plate. A European will spit them into a hand cupped as if it were holding the bottom of a glass, then he will put the pits on the plate.

- An American places his knife and fork side by side on the plate to signal that he is done with his meal, while a European often crosses them.

- When toasting someone in Europe, don't clink the glasses together. Do look the other person squarely in the eye as you sip.

- Note that most Europeans do not order coffee with the meal, but drink it afterwards. Coffee tends to be very strong.

GOOD (BUT LESS FASHIONABLE) RESTAURANTS

You really don't have to splurge to eat well in Europe. After all, most Europeans don't eat in the fancier places, but they still demand quality for their money. And they get it.

Signs of a good restaurant

- Look for a menu (in the native language) posted outside near the entrance. This will make it easy for you to judge both the food and the price range before going in. Places with good food and charm often have menus written out in longhand. Specialties change daily, and this is the easiest way for the restaurant to keep up with them.

- Look for a series of set-price meals on the menu. In Europe, it's common to see four or five set-price meals on a menu. A set-price meal will include an hors d'oeuvre, a main dish (or two), vegetable, salad, dessert, bread, and so on. You won't pay for these items separately or **à la carte.**

- Look for well-dressed clientele with a sprinkling of businessmen.

- A well-lit interior—cozy and cheerful.

- Lots of people during the main meal hours.

- Only one or two waitresses working, because the restaurant's small and intimate.

- Good, moderately priced wines.

- Cloth napkins.

- Flowers simply arranged in inexpensive vases.

Cutting the cost of meals

- Eat your main meal at lunch. You'll enjoy the same food at a fraction of the price you'd pay in the evening.

- When a menu lists several separate but similar dishes, order the least expensive dish. The more expensive dishes are usually a snare for tourists and snobs.

- Share a meal with a friend, if you're really strapped. Just ask for another plate. You'll be charged a small extra fee for this service.

- Ask the waiter whether the restaurant serves half portions. If it does, you'll cut the cost of the meal considerably.

- Don't order the same dish as someone else at your table, if you're both hearty eaters. If you both order crab, they'll often split the crab in two. If only one of you orders crab, they'll give that person the whole thing.

- Follow the drinking habits of the area in which you're traveling. Replace cocktails with a local drink.

- In modest restaurants, ask for a house, ordinary, open, local, table, or regional wine. These terms refer to wine served in carafes (pitchers). Carafes come in one-quarter, one-half, and one-liter sizes. You may have to use sign language to indicate what you want.

- Avoid ordering a rosé for "split parties." Order a bottle of red and a bottle of white. For those who want rosé, blend the two in a glass—that's how it's done. Note too that most sparkling wines (**Schaumwein, spumant, spumante**) are inferior and overpriced.

- Skip soft drinks, butter, and ice. Most Europeans go without these "luxury" items. When you see the prices, so will you!

- Skip coffee at the end of a meal, if you can, because it's very expensive.

Saving on tips

In most European restaurants, a service charge is added to the bill, so check to see if it's there before leaving an additional tip.

- If you see something like **"service compris"** or **"servizio compreso"** written on the menu itself, the tip is included in the prices listed, and the waiter should not add any further charges to the bill. Check it, however, since many waiters make conscientious efforts to dupe American tourists.

- If you see **"service non compris,"** **"service en sus,"** or **"service net"** on the menus, service is not included.

- If you're not sure whether the service charge is included in the listed prices, just ask.

Cover charges

In many restaurants, you pay what is known as a cover charge. Sometimes it's included in the listed prices, sometimes it's not.

- Look for **"couvert,"** **"coperto,"** or **"cubeirto"** noted somewhere on the menu.

- Even if you don't find these words, ask the waiter whether there is any cover charge.

Watching out for con games

Most restaurants are reputable businesses. But a lot of money can be made by fleecing unsuspecting tourists—so beware.

- Avoid places with tour buses waiting outside, or any establishment that hires a food pimp to stand in the doorway and usher you in! Good places don't have to be sold.

- If a waiter tells you that there are no set-price meals today, despite what the menu out front says, get up and leave the restaurant. That menu is a trap for tourists, since **à la carte** prices will be higher.

- Bait and switch techniques are common worldwide. One of the most common: "We don't have the dish you ordered, but we do have one just like it." Ask for the cost of the new dish!

- If a waiter places unsolicited gifts on the table, such as butter or unordered hors d'oeuvres, ask him how much they cost. If the cost seems unreasonable, send them back.

- Some waiters write the bill on the table cloth (really made of paper) or blurt out a figure after mental gyrations lasting a minute or more. To avoid being overcharged, add the bill up yourself. You might make a mental note of the approximate cost while ordering.

- If you think someone has overcharged you, say, "The last time I was here the wine (or whatever item) was less expensive." If they've made an error, they'll excuse themselves and change the price.

PICNICS

A long-time favorite form of entertainment, the picnic is one of the best ways to keep food costs down in Europe. Europeans avoid the high cost of dining-car food by doing this on trains—so why not give it a try? Naturally, if you picnic on the roadside, be sure to get well off the shoulder, to avoid possible accidents and a fine.

Shopping for supplies

You'll find most kinds of food in supermarkets, although in smaller towns you may have to go to several shops to get what you need. Each shop will specialize in one product: baked goods, meats, cheeses, produce, wine, and so on. Foods will be sold in metric measures (a kilo, made up of 1,000 grams, is equivalent to 2.2 pounds; a liter is about a quart).

- Never buy picnic food in train stations. Go to a nearby market where prices will be much lower.
- Carry a fishnet or plastic bag with you, since many smaller stores won't provide bags.

Buying bread

- Try to buy bread early in the morning when it is warm and fresh. Since these breads go stale quickly, buy only the amount you'll need.
- Ask to have a larger loaf cut in two if you won't need it all. You'll pay for the half loaf only!
- To prevent bread from going stale, wrap it loosely in a moist towel.

Buying meat and cheese

- Meat will often be sliced to your specification. You can either specify a certain number of slices or an exact weight total.
- Whenever you buy meat in a shop, ask for a little less than you think you'll need. Butchers **always** cut extra, knowing that no one will refuse meat that's already been cut!
- As with fresh bread, you may have trouble with cheese

drying out. Wrap it loosely in a towel moistened lightly with vinegar.

• Some cheeses, like Camembert and Brie, taste best **au point**, a French expression meaning creamy in the center. However, these cheeses should be stored in a plastic bag, or the aroma will overpower you as they ripen.

Buying produce

• Don't be intimidated into buying poor produce just because the owner decides to stuff bruised apples in your bag—but don't offend the owner by fingering too much of his stock.

Buying wine

In some wine shops, you'll find huge casks from which you can buy wine in varying degrees (**degrés**) of quality. The better the wine, the more expensive it is. Although the French can, you won't be able to tell the difference yourself, except between the worst and the best.

• Choose the middle wine.

• Always ask to taste these wines. Some of them may have gone bad. Do the same when buying large flasks of wine (as in Italy).

• Supply your own bottle, if you can. If you don't have one, they'll give you one at a small charge.

• Never discard bottles, since you'll get a refund for turning them back in. And never cross a border without returning bottles, since they may not be accepted in another country.

• If you forget to bring a bottle opener, don't despair or use your teeth. Just twist a key or small coin under the metal folds of the cap until they start to bend out. Keep moving the key around the base of the cap until it pops off. It takes a little time, but it works.

• If you forget to bring a corkscrew, push two nails or sharp objects into the cork. Place any long metal object between them and twist. This device will work, though not as well as a corkscrew.

NATIONAL SPECIALTIES AND CUSTOMS

Every country has its characteristic ways with food. During your travels, don't miss opportunities to taste special dishes! The following list is by no means exhaustive, but **bon appetit**, anyway.

Austria

Austrians are world famous for their pastries and desserts.

- Savor the local custom of **Jause**, a midafternoon snack, at a coffeehouse. Coffeehouses have become an Austrian institution, a kind of social and intellectual meeting place, where you can sample a dozen varieties of coffee, including Turkish, which is "hot as hell, sweet as love, and twice as black as night."

Belgium

Over a hundred Michelin rating stars have gone to Belgian restaurants, including one of the rare three-star places outside France (the Villa Lorraine in Brussels).

- Try **moules**, steamed mussels prepared in a variety of ways. Use one of the shells as a pincer to pull out the meat from the other shells—a European custom that works perfectly.

- Try some of the Ardennes ham, if you get a chance!

- Eat at a country inn. Many rural inns boast kitchens that would do France justice. Some of them are in the **relais de campagne** chain. Call Two World Tours, 800-221-4547 or write the French National Tourist Office in New York (see p. 23) for a pamphlet which includes simple maps and up-to-date prices.

- Try French fries and Belgian mayonnaise.

Denmark

Don't leave Denmark without trying a smorgasbord. Danish smorgasbords, a cold table of Danish specialties with such delicacies as fresh herring and local cheese, are well worth a splurge. They are generally served at lunch, and follow a specific pattern, which you should observe. A smorgasbord can fill an afternoon and even the largest empty stomach.

- When your waiter comes to your table, give him your order for **schnapps** for the first course and beer thereafter. You can substitute apple juice or soft drinks for both, if you prefer nonalcoholic drinks. Etiquette demands that you have something to drink with the meal, even though it jacks up the bill.

- Take your plate to the buffet and serve yourself any amount of herring and fish you want—but only these, nothing else. Then return to your table and enjoy them. When you're done with the fish, leave your plate on the table and get a new one from the buffet table. You can return as often as you like within any course, but you can't circle back to a previous one.

w serve yourself salads and cold meats—as little or as ıch as you'd like. When you've eaten them, leave your ρ,ᴜte behind once again and try the hot dishes on a new, clean plate.

- Follow the same procedure for the finale, the cheese and fruit. When you've finished this dessert, the waiter will appear to take your order for coffee. (Note that the fellow has been around all along, removing dirty plates from the table.)

- Other treats: **smørrebrød** (open-faced sandwiches), **fadøl** (draft beer), and **wienerbrød** (pastry). Milk's a steal, too.

- Don't confuse **kr** ("kroner"—Danish money) for **kl** ("hour") when you read Danish menus.

- In the countryside, stop in at one of the rural inns known as **kroer** (**kro** is singular). You'll sample typical Danish fare, from freshly sliced smoked salmon to just-caught shrimp.

France

- Sunday lunch in France is similar in popularity to our Saturday night dinners out. Without a reservation you'll have a tough time getting into a restaurant. The French dress up for this special occasion. You should too.

- When driving into the countryside, carry a list of the **relais de campagne**. These little inns are noted for superb food and service. Get the brochure by calling Two World Tours, 800-221-4547, or writing the French National Tourist Office in New York (see p. 23). It's got full information, including simple maps.

- Few French drink cocktails, considered much too hard a drink to begin a meal. If you order a martini, you'll be served vermouth with a Martini label. Don't make a scene. It's delicious!

- Bread and **croissants** (crescent rolls) are equally delicious when newly baked. You'll get them with your Continental breakfast.

- In France you'll discover over 500 varieties of cheese. Note that, when you're served cheese on a platter, you should always leave the cheese in the same shape as when it came to you (triangles should still be triangles). It is considered very poor manners to do otherwise!

- Always feel free to sample a number of varieties of cheese when in a restaurant. Ask for a small piece (**un petit morceau**) of three or four. There's no extra charge.

- Soup, omelets, **steak frites** (steak with French fries), **yaourt** (yogurt)—these cost **very** little in most French restaurants and are excellent!

- In many small French restaurants, you mix your own dressing from ingredients provided on the table. Pour several spoonfuls of oil on a dish, mix in a little vinegar and a bit of mustard. Sprinkle with salt and pepper. Now mix thoroughly and pour over the salad.

- When eating fondue in France, the custom is to kiss the person next to you if you drop bread or meat into the pot. (Men and women sit alternately around the table.) You also buy a bottle of wine for the group.

- The famous fish soup **bouillabaisse** is made only for two or more people. You'll find that it's fantastic in Marseilles.

- French fries are rarely served with catsup. You'll be offered mustard, vinegar, or fresh mayonnaise in most instances. Again, **vive la différence!**

- Popcorn, only recently popular, comes sugared unless you ask for salt (**du sel**).

- An exception to the rule that lunch is a bargain: meals are more expensive at noon in Nice.

- Many French foods are seasoned with garlic. To cut the aftertaste and reduce bad breath, eat cheese and a couple of sugar cubes drenched in crême de menthe at the end of a meal.

Germany

- Expect excellent cooking in any of the Romantik Hotels and Restaurants. These charming inns offer regional cooking at its best (see p. 62). The same is true for the castle hotels, combining old-world atmosphere with outstanding local cuisine (see p. 60).

- You'll find typical restaurants in most towns offering peasant fare: rough bread (just baked), sausages, sauerkraut, schnitzel, and home brew. Very reasonably priced.

- You'll find that the food in most German railroad stations is surprisingly good.

- Remember that, when it comes to food, the **Wurst** is best in Germany.

- When you're offered a large radish in a beerhall, try it. You pay for the radish, cover it with salt, and when the water pours out, you eat it.

ain

breakfasts are usually outstanding with everything from porridge to eggs and bacon. The latter is usually served on the undercooked side. If you want it crisp, ask for burnt bacon or bacon American-style.

- Otherwise, avoid "traditional English" fare—it's still not very good. Instead, sample foreign cooking! The exceptions are noted below.

- Don't think that pubs only offer good beer. Many of them serve snacks and full meals as well—at reasonable prices. Steak and kidney pie is a staple, usually filling and nicely prepared at the right price.

- If you want something milder than straight beer in a pub, ask for a shandy. You'll get beer and something similar to 7-Up mixed together.

- Splurge in London by trying one of the East Indian spots that offer spicy cooking—a real change of pace that'll curl your hair.

- Join the British for tea from 3:45 to 5:45 p.m. daily. Dress up and do it right at the following London hotels: Brown's, the Connaught, the Dorchester, the Hyde Park, the Ritz, the Royal Lancaster, or the Savoy.

- Ask for a serviette when you want a napkin; otherwise, you will have ordered a diaper.

- The term **rare** for meat translates to mean slightly pink or well-done. Ask for your meat **bloody**, a term that will pale many an intrepid waiter's face.

Greece

Everyone admits that there is language barrier, so don't be surprised when you're asked to go into the kitchen to pick out your lunch or dinner. Without putting your finger in the pot, point out the dish you'd like to eat.

- Meal hours are late by American standards. Lunch begins at 1:00 p.m. and goes to 4:00 p.m. Dinner begins about 10:00 p.m. and stretches to midnight (more or less).

- Take an afternoon snack, as many Greeks do, at cafés, since dinner is late. You don't have to eat and run at these places; you can dawdle all you want. Try some of the sweets.

- Don't expect to leave large tips in Greece, but do leave token tips. The tip for the waiter goes directly on the plate, while the busboy's gratuity should be left on the table.

- In Athens, you can get something close to an American coffee by asking for Nescafé.

Ireland

No one goes to Ireland for its cuisine. The food's just as good and just as bad as English food, so the same advice applies.

- Eat a big breakfast in the morning—porridge, eggs, bacon, sausage, soda bread, tea. It may be the best meal you'll get all day.

- Head for the nearest pub and have a sandwich or some oxtail soup for lunch. If you want a big meal, have it at noon, since Irish restaurants serve only light dinners in the evening. And if you do go to a fancy restaurant for dinner, be sure to try the salmon.

- Guinness stout, is, of course, the national drink. It's rich, dark, foamy, and somewhat bitter, and in Ireland it's served at room temperature. Give it a chance.

- You'll never drink alone in an Irish pub. Someone will soon join you and buy you a drink. In fact, it's an Irish custom to buy drinks for everyone in the group, and you'll be expected to do likewise. By the end of the evening (pubs close at 11:30), you're likely to have a line of drinks waiting for your attention.

Italy

- In most restaurants, pick the table that suits you and sit down. Then look at the closest waiter for a nonverbal sign of approval. If the table is reserved (which is rare), he'll point you to another one nearby.

- You are not expected to order a full meal right from the start, although you can if you prefer. Italians frequently order only one dish at a time, **à la carte.**

- You'll often find displays of food at the entrance to a restaurant. If you don't understand the menu, you can always point to things you'd like.

- You can expect a surcharge for the music of a local band or symphony at a restaurant or café.

- Make a meal of spaghetti, which Italians consider to be no more than an antipasto or warm-up dish. Italians eat less sauce on their spaghetti than Americans do. If you want more, ask for some (**"Più di salsa, per favore"**). Meatballs aren't served with spaghetti in Italy.

- **Al pomodoro** means "with tomato"; **alla Bolognese,** "with meat"; **al vongole,** "with clams." **Scallopine** refers to slices of veal, **salsa** or **sugo** is "sauce," and **al dente** is "slightly chewy" (of pasta).

- Italian pizza disappoints many Americans, because it's crusty and served cool (almost cold). In many pizza spots, you can buy it by the slice. You pay by weight.

- Italy is one place in Europe where you can get excellent ice cream—and enough of it!

Netherlands

- If you're trying to keep costs down, look for an emblem with a fork on it in restaurant windows. This is a symbol for a restaurant serving tourist menus. About six hundred such restaurants are found in Holland.

- You'd be crazy to leave the Netherlands without trying the Indonesian **rijsttafel** (rice table), consisting of a dozen or more dishes laid out for one of the world's greatest culinary adventures. It's a symphony of food, very expensive but worth every florin.

- Seafood tends to be vastly overpriced. Herring's the exception. When the herring comes in, the Dutch go wild, chomping it down right in the streets together with bits of onion spread on rough bread.

Norway

- Simple continental breakfasts are often included in room prices. Some hotels serve larger, more typical Norwegian fare which may include a morning **smørgåsbørd** with everything from sliced tomatoes and cucumbers to pickled herring and sardines. **Rømmegbrøt**, a filling, fattening porridge, may be difficult to enjoy, though it's authentic.

- Breakfast may include many varieties of milk, some of which are similar to sour cream or buttermilk. For "normal" milk ask simply for **melk**. When in doubt, sample a small amount first. But remember that many Norwegians prefer buttermilk on their cereal!

- Norwegians tend to eat a light snack for lunch. A heavier, more satisfying meal is served in the late afternoon or early evening from 4 to 6 p.m. It's a better buy than lunch in most restaurants.

- For a coffee break try **vaffler**, traditional waffles that are served cold.

- You'll find excellent peasant food in **caffestova**, coffee rooms with hearty cuts of meat, fresh potatoes and vegetables—all served in simple surroundings at reasonable prices. Such places are not oriented to tourists; that's the reason they're such an exceptional value. They're often tucked away on second floors with only a simple sign on a first floor door or side of a building. Ask for the nearest **caffestova** if you're having trouble locating one.

• Open-faced sandwiches, **smørbrød**, are served in simple cafes and fancier restaurants as well. Extremely popular and very tasty—don't leave without trying them.

• Beer can be quite expensive, but often is the only practical choice.

• Some other specialties most Americans enjoy: fresh trout or salmon (expensive but excellent); shrimp and crayfish, popular along the coast and in southern Norway; reindeer steak, usually served as a specialty in fancier restaurants and simply outstanding; any of the preserves which taste almost like fresh fruit; goat cheese; and multer berries, beige mountain berries, as expensive as they are distinctive in taste.

Portugal

The government supports a network of country inns (**pousadas**) throughout the country. Rooms in these inns are a great value, and so are meals. The latter offer regional specialties and drinks at bargain prices.

You'll be pushed into hearing **fado**, wailing love songs sung by black-shawled women in night clubs. The **fado**'s fascinating; the food's generally not.

• Wherever you hear **fado**, you'll pay a social security tax on the total amount of the bill. Keep it small.

• Chicken and seafood are the staples, along with potatoes and rice. The latter are served with everything, so ask for green vegetables or salad to break up the monotony.

• Try the chicken **piri-piri**, spicy and delicious.

• Also sample the seafood and beer combination offered in **cervejarias**. Noisy, informal, jammed—but great.

• Try the **cataplana** if you get to the Algarve—an excellent stew.

• Savor the almond sweets, too. This area is one of the main almond-producing regions in the world.

Spain

• Throughout Spain, you'll find **paradores**, inns that offer both rooms and meals at reasonable prices. You can get a list of these inns from the Spanish National Tourist Office (see p. 23) or call Iberia Airlines.

- Meal hours in Spain are late. Lunch from 2 to 3 p.m., dinner from 10 p.m. to midnight (earlier by an hour or so in the winter). If you want to rub elbows with the Spanish, you must change your eating habits.

- If you want to try typical or regional cooking, ask for a nearby **tasca** or **restaurante tipico**. You may have a language barrier once inside, but the food will be worth the effort—both interesting and reasonably priced.

- Join the locals in sampling **tapas**, snacks found on the counters of bars and small restaurants. Order a glass of wine, which is generally delivered with something to nibble on. If you're with a group of hungry people and want a larger order of any particular item, ask for **una racion**. Don't be afraid to use sign language; just point to whatever food you want!

- Fish is one of the most reliable dishes throughout most of Spain, particularly along the coast. Obviously, it's best if **pescada fresco** or fresh fish. Ask if in doubt!

- Don't bother ordering beef. It won't measure up to your expectations.

- Sweets, liqueurs and cheese will cut through the odor and aftertaste of garlic.

- The safest choice for dessert: fresh fruit, usually ripe and juicy. Peel it. **Flan**, a custard with caramel sauce, can be a good choice in more expensive restaurants but something to avoid in lesser places. Note that pastries in Spain are not as sweet as you're used to, but they're something you'll want to try anyway.

- For an inexpensive breakfast or late afternoon snack from 6 to 7 p.m., try **churros**, thin, round doughnuts or **porra**, thick, straight doughnuts—neither of which are as sweet as our version. You dunk them in **café con leche** (coffee and milk) or hot chocolate (**chocolate**), the latter very thick and creamy. You find these in bars or small cafes.

- **Paella**, bits of fish and meat smothered in saffron rice, should be on your must-try list. It takes forty thousand blossoms of an autumn crocus to make one pound of saffron—which explains why saffron is so expensive.

- **Arroz**, rice, is a staple.

- Stick to red wines throughout much of Spain but give the white ones a chance in Barcelona.

- **Sangria**, a fruit-filled punch made of different wines, is sweetened with sugar or honey and served in an ice-filled pitcher.

- In the northwestern region around Oviedo, try the local apple cider **cidra**, somewhat similar to Champagne and poured with a flourish from a bottle held high above the glass—a real show.

- In Galicia, north of Portugal, don't miss the **ribeiro** wine, sour with lots of body.

- If you prefer drinks with a mild alcoholic content, ask for wine or beer **con gaseosa**. The drink will come mixed with charged water similar to 7-Up in taste.

- A special treat: if you're in Madrid during the summer, try a **leche merengada**, frozen milk and egg whites sprinkled with cinnamon. If you would like it flavored with coffee, ask for a **blanco e negro.**

- Also cold and a summer drink, but more unusual with a flavor similar to that of coconut: **horchata**. It originates in the area around Valencia, but can be found in other areas as well.

Wales

- At pubs, order food at the bar and carry it self-service style to your table.

- Our beer is called "lager" in Wales.

- Lamb and mutton dishes are a treat.

DRINKING GUIDE

Europe is filled with special drinks, from **schnapps** and **slivovitz** to **genever** and **grappa**. Start off with a few drinks of **aquavit**, chilled in the snow until it's so cold it slides down your throat like a chip of ice; or sip the licorice-tasting **pastis**, which turns cloudy with a splash of water or piece of ice; or try chugging **aguardente**, favorite of Portuguese fishermen, while you watch it burn holes in the deck where you spilled it.

Cutting costs on drinks

- Always bring a bottle of booze into Scandinavia, where costs are astronomical! And stick to local specialties wherever else you go—imports are always expensive.

- Eschew minuscule drinks served between acts at London theaters, popping around the corner to a local pub for a real drink instead.

- Avoid ordering individual drinks if you're in a group at nightclubs. Ask for the price of the least expensive bottle of wine, to be shared by all at the table.

Local peculiarities

- Order a double (for which you'll pay double) in England to end up with something similar to a shot of booze.

- When sampling a smorgasbord (see p. 129), you're expected to gulp, not sip, the **aquavit**: if you let it warm up, you'll be able to taste it (and you don't want to).

- **Genever**, a Dutch liquor, comes in two strong forms: **oud** (old) and **jong** (young). Both of them could peel varnish off a table.

- Port wine is always passed to the left (port vs. starboard?)—even if the person who wants it is sitting to your immediate right.

For wine lovers

- Head immediately for France, Germany, Italy, Portugal, Austria and Spain. Great Britain, Greece, Hungary, Switzerland and Yugoslavia have limited wine production, too.

- White wines are the best buy in Germany; reds are the best buy in France and Italy.

- Try the young Austrian wines (**Heurige**) in early May. Places serving these wines hang a sprig of evergreen from the eaves.

- You may not care for the resin in the wine in Greece. If that's the case, ask for **aretsinoto krasi**, unresinated wine.

- In Sicily, drink bottled wines only (Segesta, Marsala, Corvo Malvasia).

- Try a very interesting Portuguese wine, **vinho verde**, which is consumed young and cool. It comes from the northern part of the country and is often overlooked by travelers.

Sampling drinks and wines for free

Wherever liquor and liqueurs are made, you can take a tour of the distillery and sample the results for free. One of the most popular tours is in Cognac, where the authentic brandy known as "the heart of wine" is made.

- A well-marked, sixty-two-mile-long trail winds its way through Scotland from one distillery to another, for those who would like to sample some of the world's great scotches.

- In northern Portugal, you'll find the **entrepôts** for Port wine at Vila Nova de Gaia, the town across the river from Oporto. You'll be able to sample everything from newly fashionable white Ports to thirty-year-old tawnies.

- Not quite free, but very inexpensive, are the Port wines served at the Vinho do Porto do Solar, Rua Sâo Pedro Alcantara 42, Lisbon. Ask the concierge for a map showing its exact location in the center of town.

- Throughout France, you can sample free wines wherever you see the sign "**Dégustation gratuite.**" It would be hard to drive anywhere without seeing several of these.

- To sample Champagne, try the **caves** of Épernay, and Reims.

- For Italian wines, head to the Bolla Vineyards near Verona.

- And for Spanish sherries, try the **bodegas** (Gonzales, Byass and Company, Ltd.) near Cadiz.

For beer lovers

Most breweries offer tours and free beer to participants. Very popular are the Tuborg (Copenhagen) and Heineken (Amsterdam) tours. And don't be prejudiced by what you've heard and read about German beers being the best. They're fabulous, but so are Belgian and British brews.

- Order tap instead of bottled beer whenever you can. It comes out in a frosty, froth-covered mug containing a quarter-, a half-, or a full liter of brew. To show the amount of beer you want, just point to the size glass (mug) you'd like.

- **Tap beer** in five languages: **bière à pression** (French), **Bier vom Fass** (German), **birra del barril** (Italian), **cerveza de (en) barril** (Spanish), **cerveja a late (a giraffa)** (Portuguese).

- Always ask for **export öl** in Scandinavia, to get beer with more than a smidgeon of alcohol.

- Look for beer halls (**cervejarias**) in Spain and Portugal where you can wash down many types of shellfish with ice cold beer.

- Don't worry about brand names in Germany, where every hamlet produces exquisite beer. Stick with the local brew!

- Try pub-crawling, one of the most popular forms of entertainment in Great Britian. It consists of sampling many beers in many pubs during the evening. Pubs (locals) offer fabulous people-watching and suddenly become "private"—for whoever's still left inside—at closing time. Note that pubs close from about 2:30 p.m. to 6:00 p.m. daily.

Basics on water

- The water in the WC (toilet) of a train is not drinkable. Bring your own in a flask. That's what the Europeans do, since the cost for bottled water on trains is unbelievably high.

- You'll find faucets for drinking water in train stations and nearby parks. If you've forgotten to bring a flask, buy water or juice by the bottle in stores near the station. It will be very reasonable.

- In some restaurants you'll find carafes of tap water on the table, for which there is no charge. Do what the locals do and drink it ... unless you espy unusual forms of aquatic life in the bottle.

- If there is no water on the table, you'll have to ask for it. Ask for tap water to avoid the charges for bottled mineral water. Here's **tap water** in five languages: **l'eau du robinet** (French), **Leitungswasser** (German), **l'acqua du rubinetto** (Italian), **a agua a torneira** (Portuguese), **la aqua del grifo** (Spanish).

- If you order mineral water, waiters will ask you whether you want mineral water with or without **gaz**, or carbonation. If you don't want fizzy water, shake your head and say **no gaz**. This pidgen talk will get the message across.

- If a waiter brings an open bottle of mineral water to your table, send it back. European custom demands that the bottle be opened at the table.

Soft and cold drinks

- Cold milk is a common drink in Holland, Scandinavia, northern Germany, and Great Britain. Skip it in other areas (or buy it in grocery stores). Beer could really be considered a soft drink in parts of Scandinavia, since the alcohol content is minimal.

- The inflated price of soft drinks in restaurants eventually discourages most Americans from drinking them abroad. However, bottled soft drinks, sold by the liter in grocery stores, are quite reasonable.

14

GETTING AROUND

Inter-European travel can be quite complex. It would be a good idea to read about the modes of transportation you've chosen for traveling around Europe before you go abroad. Then refresh your memory by reading it one more time at the beginning of your trip.

FLYING

Most of the ideas that will help you enjoy plane travel to the fullest have been covered in earlier sections. However, here are some hints that are most pertinent to flying around Europe.

Departure taxes

In some countries, you'll have to pay a departure tax at the airport when you check in. This is one good way of using up spare change. However, it can be extremely frustrating if you have to cash a traveler's check (and lose on the exchange) just to pay this tax.
- Ask the airline ahead of time whether you'll be subject to such a tax on departure.

ARRANGING FOR CARS

Having your own car will offer you great flexibility; however, you'll need to know a few details to prevent trouble when arranging to pick one up in Europe.

Picking up a new car at the factory

- In addition to the basic documents, get the **Green Card** for insurance, the **registration card** as proof of ownership and a **nationality sticker** (needed to cross borders), and the **list of service stations** that provide maintenance repairs.

- Tell the clerk that you have a first-aid kit and a triangular Danger sign, even if you don't, since prices are inflated for these items at the factory.

- Check the car over from top to bottom. Make sure everything works: the horn, wipers, lights, seats, seat belts, etc.

- Ask the clerk to show you how to work the jack. (This is a good way to make sure there is one and that it works.) Check on the spare tire: take it out and look at it carefully.

- Give the car a quick check to make sure all fluids are up to the Full mark. Don't assume anything is right.

- Get a good road map, if you haven't already done so.

- Have the car filled up. (The factory will give you just enough gas to let you get to the pump outside, and sometimes less than that.)

- Ask for directions to the road leading you to your first destination. This one step can save you an hour or more of aggravation!

Car insurance

- Insure your car through the factory for the shortest time permissible. For longer trips abroad, extend the coverage through a private European insurance company. If you're on a short trip, accept the fact that insurance will be a rip-off: you have no choice, anyway.

- You'll need a permanent address abroad if you want to extend coverage through a private company. The permanent address can be that of a friend or relative.

- Check your insurance company's Green Card, which is a kind of folder consisting of many sheets of green paper. At the bottom of each sheet, you'll see abbreviations for European countries. If any of these have been crossed out, your insurance will not be valid there.

- If you'll be traveling in any of the Scandinavian countries (Denmark, Finland, Norway, Sweden), make sure that none of their names has been crossed out. If any one name has been crossed out, your insurance will not be valid in the other countries, because of a reciprocal insurance agreement.

Buying a used car

You'll find long lines of car owners carrying placards advertising their cars in front of American Express offices, especially in the fall.

- Don't look for recent models. They cost the same (or nearly the same) as brand-new cars, when sold on an export basis.

- Make sure that all local taxes have been paid. If you buy a model slated for export, you won't have to pay them at all.

- If you're buying the car from a private party, make sure that you can legally have the insurance transferred to your name.

- Buy a car that can be serviced in the area where you'll be traveling.

- Assume that everything's going to fall apart ten minutes after you buy it, and make an offer accordingly.

Questions about Rental Cars

- What is the full car rental price for the length of time you plan to travel?
- Are there any additional taxes or service charges to pay?
- Is there an extra charge for leaving the car in another city? (Tell them where you intend to leave the car.)
- Is there an extra charge for full collision coverage? If so, what is it? Pay it. If full collision coverage isn't available in an area (as in the Azores), do not drive a rental car there. An accident and the ensuing legal hassles could keep you a prisoner in a foreign country for a long time.
- If the car breaks down, who pays for repairs?
- Do repairs have to be done in specific garages, or can they be done anywhere? If specific places are established, get a list.
- Who pays for oil, gas, and lubrication?
- Is there a documents charge?
- How much is the deposit?
- Can you pay the bill in dollars? (Great if you can.)
- What will the charge be if you should arrive later than agreed upon to return the car?
- If you cut the trip short, what will the charge be?
- If time and mileage come out to be less than the amount of your unlimited mileage agreement, will you be allowed to pay that smaller amount?
- How much is the charge per gallon for filling the car on return? You may save by filling it yourself.
- Are all the documents (Green Card and registration) in the car?
- Is there a map in the car? Is there a booklet on service stations for this make of car?
- Is the tank full of gas?
- Where's the jack? (Have them show you how it works.)
- Is there a spare tire in the car? (Check to see.)
- Are the tires in good condition? (Check by sticking a small coin into the tread to judge its depth.)

Renting a car in advance

- Make sure that you have the exact address where you are to pick up the car.

- Get a written confirmation of the arrangement in advance.

Renting a car once you arrive

Why not rent a car where it will be most economical to do so? If you will be traveling extensively by car, plan to start your trip in the country where the costs are lowest (see p. 54).

- Rates are often lower in small towns outside the main tourist destinations.

- During the off season, you can get substantial price reductions on car rental from agencies abroad. Call, or have the concierge call, several agencies to get a few comparative prices. Savings at smaller agencies can range from 25 to 50 percent off the large companies' prices. (Be sure to tip the concierge for his efforts!)

- Rent small cars, which are better in every way. They slurp up less gas, are plenty roomy if you're traveling reasonably light, can go anywhere, can weasel into tiny parking spots, and cost less on fees for ferries and toll roads.

- Unlimited mileage agreements at a set cost per week are usually your best bet.

- In some areas, there are age limitations on applicants for car rental. These vary from age twenty-three on the low end to age seventy on the high end.

Selling a car abroad

If you bought a used car abroad, you will already have paid all local taxes. When it comes time to sell the car, you can sell it to anybody you want without paying further taxes.

If you bought a car slated for export to the U.S., however, you will have purchased it free of local taxes. If you then sell the car, you'll be obliged to pay all of them—and they can amount to hundreds of dollars. The solution: sell the car to another American who intends to export it to the U.S. Here's how to do it.

- Give that person the registration papers, the Green Card (for insurance), and a signed note stating that the person may use the car and cross any border with it. Insurance will be no problem, since no restrictions can be placed on liability coverage. This means that anyone can drive the car as long as it's insured.

- Hand that person a note saying that you have sold him the car. Leave the date of sale open to be filled in with a date later than your date of arrival in the U.S. The other person will pay you for the car. This procedure definitely stretches legality—but why should you pay tax on a car that is going to be exported anyway?

- If you sell the car to a foreigner who does not intend to export it, either you or he must pay the taxes; there is no way around it.

Shipping a car to the U.S.

There's only one word to describe this whole process—pain.

- Note: shipping rates vary, but nothern ports are generally less expensive.

- Ask the manufacturer about reduced rates from specific ports.

- Make sure that the shipping cost estimate includes such services as draining the gas tank, steam cleaning the car, and waxing it (for protection against salt).

- Buy marine insurance.

- Arrive at the pier with as little gas as possible, since the gas tank will be drained.

- In the U.S., you'll have to clear the car through customs or pay an agent to do it. Either way, you'll pay duty and a handling charge.

- If you leave the car in storage for more than three days, you'll pay a daily storage charge.

- Brace yourself for a dock strike, which may delay the unloading of your car.

DRIVING

A car gives you much better access to the undeveloped areas of Europe than you have with other means of travel. But driving does have its drawbacks. You will have a lot to adjust to, and a lot to remember about driving laws and customs. For the adventurous, though, nothing beats it!

Gas

On the Continent, gas is usually sold by the liter (a little more than a quart). In Great Britain, it's usually sold by the imperial gallon (about five quarts). Prices may be double the pump total in some areas.

- Since gas station hours and days of business are unpredictable, play it safe and try not to get too low on gas.

- Note that European gas stations often charge for services like inflating tires, cleaning windshields, and checking the oil. Ask for such services—or do them yourself.

- In warm weather, buy gas in the early morning or late in the evening. You'll get more gas when it's cool out.

- Fill up especially frequently when you're in Spain, Portugal, Yugoslavia, Greece, Norway, Sweden, or any of the islands. Open gas stations are long distances apart in these areas.

- Supergrade gas (ninety-five octane) is generally worth the extra cost.

- Always ask for a specific amount of gas, or the attendant may try to squeeze every last cent out of you.

- Fill up before crossing a border into a country where gas costs more. The following countries are listed in order of **increasing** gas prices: Spain, West Germany, Netherlands, Austria, Switzerland, Norway, Ireland, Great Britain, Denmark, Luxembourg, Belgium, Finland, Portugal, Italy, France, Sweden.

Italian gas coupons

In Italy, you can cut gas costs by getting a **Carta Carburante Turistica**, which allows you to buy special coupons. This card is sporadically available to motorists driving a car with non-Italian plates (a good reason to rent or buy a car outside of Italy, if you plan extensive travel there).

- Get the card as you cross the border into Italy.

- Use the card to buy coupons for a set number of gallons, allotted on a per diem basis. These coupons are available from the Automobile Club of Italy, which has offices in most major Italian towns. They are also available from the Banco Nazionale del Lavoro, 25 West 51st Street, New York, NY 10018.

- To get coupons you'll also need the registration number of your car.

When the gas tank is empty

- When the gas tank is empty, use the mileage marathon technique: accelerate as slowly as possible to twenty miles per hour, then immediately turn off the ignition while moving into neutral gear. Let the car slow down to five miles per hour. Start the engine again and repeat the same steps. This technique can double and even triple gas mileage in an emergency!

- If your steering wheel locks when the ignition is off, this technique will not work. It's also not recommended for steep downhill grades—but you may have to take a gamble. Finally, it's illegal in some areas—but, late at night on a deserted road, you won't really care!

- If you have to stop, don't race the engine.

- If the car won't stop running when you turn off the ignition, pop it dead in gear (not very good for the car, but you'll save gas).

- Don't allow the car to sway from side to side: this will save you one to two miles per gallon.

Road travel

The only fast roads in Europe are the superhighways. Other roads can be tied up by traffic, trucks (belching diesel smoke), repairs, mopeds, and even herds of goats.

Coastal and mountain roads must follow the natural contours of the hills, meaning hundreds of curves per mile. Passing is virtually impossible on many of these highways. You move as slowly as the slowest link in the chain.

- Start trips early and end them early.

- Try to average no more than 250 miles per day; even that's quite a bit.

- Do just the opposite of what most Europeans do. Instead of taking a break for lunch, drive between noon and 2:00 p.m. in order to take advantage of better traffic conditions.

- Avoid driving in cities. City traffic is almost always impossible, except on Sundays. On weekdays, if you must drive in cities at all, avoid morning and evening rush hours.

Maps

Good maps can make a trip an enjoyable, rather than a frustrating, experience.

- Select maps to conform with the kind of travel you are planning. Why buy expensive, detailed maps if you'll only be traveling between major cities? On the other hand, you'll appreciate such detail when you are exploring some rural area.

- Many of the foreign automobile and touring clubs offer very good maps; those of the Touring Club of Italy are excellent.

- AAA (American Automobile Association) maps will do quite well for all but the most detailed data. They're free to members.

- The Michelin maps, available in most bookstores abroad, are reliable. Make sure they're up to date (dates are printed on the cover of the map).

- In Great Britain, you can buy ordnance maps, extremely detailed for off-the-beaten-path trips. In Ireland, look for Geodetic Survey maps.

Driving Customs in Europe

This chart outlines some of the regional peculiarities that you'll run into abroad. Note that you must wear a seat belt in most European countries and that children under twelve should be placed in the back seat, according to local ordinances.

Austria	Don't drink and drive—not even one drink! Have chains for winter driving. In the mountains, cars going up hill have priority. Driving is slow in most areas.
Belgium	You must wear a seat belt. Watch for cyclists—thousands of them. Exceedingly slow driving.
Denmark	Stiff penalties for drinking and driving. Many ferries. Parking on the right side of the road only. Slow driving.
Finland	Stiff penalties for drinking and driving. Fill up frequently—don't get caught without gas. Have low beams on from September 1 to April 30 during the day. Good, if long, driving.
France	**Always** give priority to cars on the right. Watch for mopeds and cyclists. Have chains for mountain driving in winter. Keep lights on in fog, mist, or poor light. Good driving overall.
Germany	Gas stations open all day on Autobahns. Very high speed on Autobahns. Blink lights if you want to pass someone. Slower traffic must stay on the right! Excellent driving overall.
Great Britain	Drive on the left. Slow driving overall. Leave turn signal on while passing.
Greece	Ignore horns. Watch out for flocks. Investigate gas coupons.
Ireland	Drive on the left. Tight winding roads. Watch for flocks of animals. Fill up frequently. Slow driving.
Italy	To get gas coupons, have foreign plates (don't rent a car in Italy). See p. 146. Don't park in green zones, or the car may be towed away. Charges on **autostrade** are steep.

Italy (continued)	You pay when you exit. Cars are very helpful on Isola d'Elba. No cars can go to Capri. Off-season and round-trip reductions on ferries to Sicily. Chains are required in mountains in winter. Good driving on main roads, very slow on secondary routes (bad along the coast).
Luxembourg	Tight, winding roads. Watch for cyclists. Wear a seat belt. Good driving overall.
Netherlands	Wear a seat belt. Watch for cyclists. Use major roads when in a hurry. Leave car parked in Amsterdam. Good driving overall.
Norway	Don't drink and drive. Don't speed excessively (you will lose your license). Fill up frequently. Good, if long, driving overall. A "mile" is six American miles.
Portugal	Narrow roads in many areas. Cobblestone dangerous when wet. Frequent road repairs. Fill up often when off the beaten path. Watch for flocks of animals. Slow driving.
Spain	Stick to major highways for fast driving. Roads skirting the coast are slow. Trucks are a real problem. Flash lights or sound horn to pass. Righthand blinker on is the signal to pass (all clear). Very slow driving overall.
Sweden	Don't drink and drive. Fill up frequently when off the beaten path. Good driving overall. A "mile" is six American miles.
Switzerland	Cars going up the mountain have priority. Yellow postal buses have priority (you must get over on the shoulder, in some cases). Chains are needed to cross passes in winter. Most driving is not in the mountains. Very good driving overall.
Yugoslavia	Have any dents or scratches noted in your passport, next to your visa, on entry into the country. You may be charged with an accident otherwise. Fill up frequently. The coastal route is packed during the summer. Slow driving overall.

Superhighways

Using superhighways is the fastest and most efficient way to get around in Europe. **Superhighway(s)** are called **autoroute(s)** (French), **Autobahn(en)** (German), **autostrada (autostrade)** (Italian), **auto estrada(s)** (Portuguese), and **autopista(s)** (Spanish).

- You'll have to pay tolls on many of them, but, if you're in a hurry, they'll be worth the price.

Speed limits

Maximum speeds are posted in kilometers per hour (kph) except in Great Britain, which is not on the metric system. The main difference you'll find is the high (in some cases unlimited) speeds allowed on the major freeways.

- To convert speed limits or mileage signs given in kilometers into miles, divide the figure by ten and multiply by six. For example: 80 kph ÷ 10 = 8; 8 × 6 = 48 mph.

- In areas designated for high speed, slower traffic must stay to the right. If someone approaches you from behind, you must move over to make way. Often cars coming from the rear will blink their lights as a warning signal for you to move over. Since speeds in the left lane can reach 120 to 140 miles per hour, if you do not move over, you can cause a serious accident.

Parking

One of the biggest headaches for the motorist in Europe is finding a place to park the car. You can almost always find space in a garage, but the daily charge of several dollars adds up quickly. Most people prefer to park on the street and take their chances with vandalism. if you've got an aerial, push it down. Bend-the-Aerial is a favorite European game, Break-off-the-Aerial is a popular variation.

- If you do find a parking place, take it and leave the car parked for good.

- If the place you find has a meter, take it until an unmetered parking place opens up.

- Don't put money into the meter. Accept the fact that you're going to get a ticket.

- Some people think parking tickets make good souvenirs—you'll have to decide about that for yourself.

Parking tickets

No Parking signs may be placed on the walls of buildings or painted on the walls, and are sometimes very difficult to see. Make sure you're not blocking someone's driveway, which may be closed

with an iron gate. However, keep in mind that police rarely
with foreign license plates anywhere in Europe, unless
blocking traffic or the commissioner's driveway. But don' ⌐ct
immunity from the law just because you're a foreigner.

- Do not park in green zones in Italy, especially if you're
driving a car with Italian plates. If you park in these
areas, your car will be towed away at your expense.

- Do pay the little men in Italy who stick tags on your car:
it costs about sixteen cents a park.

- Do pay the boys in Naples who hover over you like a
swarm of gnats. Give the oldest boy in the group about
fifty cents to be divided up as he sees fit. Make a motion with your hand indicating that it's to be shared (try
to give him lots of small change).

- You are supposed to use time discs in blue zones of
Europe. These discs can be obtained free of charge in
many banks, gas stations, and police stations. They
may be nuisances to get, but if you **don't** want a parking
ticket collection, you'll need them.

Moving violations

- **Don't drink and drive**—particularly in Austria, Denmark,
Finland, Norway, and Sweden, where penalties are stiff
for having had even one drink. This charge can put you
in the clink for three weeks, foreigner or not.

- If you're stopped on any charge, stay cool and show
your international driver's license. Generally, except
for drunken-driving tags, fines can be paid on the spot,
and your license can sometimes get you out of a fine
altogether. You'll be given a receipt if you must pay.

- If you are driving someone else's car, you cannot cross
borders without written permission from the car's
owner.

- If you are traveling with a minor, you cannot cross
borders without written permission from the minor's
parents.

- Follow local customs concerning headlights. Use parking lights in cities (flashing on your low beams as you
approach intersections) if others do so.

- Don't get annoyed at the French for flashing their high
beams at you when you're on low. Since they're used to
yellow fog lights, white low beams appear too bright to
them.

- Watch for a trucker's signals to pass—usually a wave
or a turn signal. Say thanks with two bips of your horn,

and otherwise leave the horn alone.

- To find city centers, look for signs saying **"centre ville"** (French) or **"centro città"** (Italian); or head for the highest visible church spire.

- Be prepared for an occasional trek into the scrub, in preference to foul (or nonexistent) bathrooms. But never choose the outside edge of a mountain trail. Those innocent-looking low bushes might really be the tops of tall trees clinging to the side of the mountain! This is not a joke; it's a warning from mountain police, who have to fetch out the bodies of unwary tourists each year.

- Always yield to traffic on the right (including pedestrians and cows), especially in France.

- Never cross white or yellow center lines.

Motorcycling strategies

- When passing long lines of cars, watch for the occasional irate motorist, who (in a fit of jealousy) will swing his door open to knock you off the road.

- Since a motorcycle can't stop as quickly as a car, leave plenty of space between you and the car in front of you.

- Stay in the center of your lane: this will discourage motorists from squeezing by you as if you were on a bicycle.

Car repairs

Repairs are generally less expensive in smaller towns. In southern European countries, repairs often cost a fraction of what they'd cost in the north.

- Always drop your car off at night to be repaired the next day. This allows the engine to cool off.

- Get an estimate in writing.

- Agree on a pickup time. Have the mechanic note it on your estimate.

Breakdowns on the road

- Members of American automobile clubs can be covered for emergency road service abroad by paying small extra fees for temporary membership in foreign clubs. Contact the AAA or other automobile clubs for full information.

- If you have a breakdown on a superhighway, lift your hood and wait—and wait and wait. Mobile road service or police will eventually come your way.

- If you're out in the boondocks, wave down a car for help. Or an oxcart, or a moped, or a . . .

- If you rent a car, ask for a list of numbers to call in case of a breakdown. Get numbers for all the areas you'll be visiting (see below).

- If you buy a new car, check in the glove compartment to make sure that there is a pamphlet listing service stations.

European Road Service

Austria	Use emergency phones placed at one-mile intervals on main roads.
Belgium	Local number for **Touring Secours VAB-VTB (Wacht op de Weg)** or **RACB.**
Denmark	Local number for **Forenede Danske Motorejere.**
Finland	Nearest filling station.
France	Local number for **Police Secours-assistance.**
Germany	Local number for **Strassenwacht.**
Great Britain	01-262-1638. Use phones placed at one-mile intervals on main highways.
Greece	107.
Ireland	Nearest filling station.
Italy	Use phones placed at one-mile intervals on **autostrade.** Ask for **Soccorso autostradale.** In other areas, dial 113 and ask for **Soccorso autostradale.**
Luxembourg	311031. Ask for **Secours automobile.**
Netherlands	Local number for **Wegenwacht** (patrols from 7:00 a.m. to 11:00 p.m.).
Norway	Local number for **Norges Automobile Forbund** (patrols from June 20 to September 1 only).
Portugal	Nearest filling station. If you break down on Ponte Abril leading into Lisbon, put a white handkerchief on the car door to signal for help.
Spain	Nearest filling station.
Sweden	Local number for **Larmtjonst AB.**
Switzerland	Use emergency phones placed at one-mile intervals on main highways.
Yugoslavia	Nearest filling station.

Car ferries

- You can get information on ferries at the American Express office in most cities.

- Watch for off-season discounts.

- Ask about round-trip discounts.

- In the peak season, try to reserve space, in order to avoid delays. If you don't have a reservation, you'll be placed on a ferry on a first-come, first-served basis.

- You can make reservations ahead of time through some railroads. Inquire at the train station.

- The smaller your car, the less you pay.

TAKING TRAINS

Whether or not you use a Eurailpass, taking trains can be a great way to get where you want to go. A few pieces of information can really help make travel go smoothly.

Validating a Eurailpass

You will have to validate your Eurailpass at the station where you start your first rail trip. Small slip-ups can cause big trouble at this point; but you can prevent them.

- Before your turn comes, write down the dates your pass will be good for. Before the clerk writes the dates on the pass, compare your dates with his. This simple double-checking procedure may save you considerable grief, since any erasures on the pass may cause it to be challenged by conductors.

- If a mistake should still occur somehow, ask the clerk to fill out a paper showing the correct validity dates. If a conductor causes problems later on, show him the slip.

- If you board a train without getting your pass validated, the conductor will do so for a three-dollar charge, which must be paid in the proper foreign currency.

Cutting costs without Eurailpasses

- Travel second class—it's 33 percent cheaper as a rule. But go first class in Greece, Italy, Portugal, and Spain, if you find second class trying.

- Make a point of asking for the least expensive fare. Check into reductions for group travel, round-trip fares, excursion fares, youth fares, one-day fares, one-week fares, one-month fares. Look into circular tours;

midweek fares; weekend fares; regional, family, gross-kilometer fares; seasonal and holiday fares; senior citizens' discounts ... Got the picture?

- Avoid taking trains that require you to pay supplemental charges. Their speed or comfort comes at a price.

Insuring the best train ride

- Get reservations for popular trains, to avoid waiting in lines (see p. 50). If you didn't make them in the U.S., make them as soon as you arrive in a city. Lines are shortest in midmornings, Monday through Thursday.

- Get a nonsmoker seat, if you don't smoke.

- Ask for a window seat, which gives you the window and also a fold-out table for writing, playing cards, or picnicking.

- When traveling to a city where you don't have a room reservation, plan to arrive on the earliest train.

Getting to train stations

In a number of cities, you'll find that there are several train stations, so that making connections can become a headache. Of course, you will have to know which train station to go to for which destination. During rush hours, use the underground (subway) whenever possible to get from one station to another. It's both expensive and painfully slow to cross cities by taxi.

Provisions for train travel

- If you want to cut costs, bring your own food and drink. You may want to bring your own water: the water in WCs on trains is not drinkable.

- Bring local currency for each country you'll travel through, if you plan to buy food or drink or to rent a **couchette** (bunk bed) on board. Buy currency at banks to get the best exchange rate.

In train stations

- Note: European train schedules use the military (twenty-four-hour) system of time; so that 12.00 means noon, and 24.00 means midnight. The system is designed to keep you from confusing 5:00 a.m. (5.00) with 5:00 p.m. (17.00).

- Ask a native speaker to pronounce the name of your destination in the appropriate foreign language, so that you will be able to recognize it over the public address system when it is announced.

- If you have lots of luggage, look for pushcarts, which are free—but usually scarce. If your cart won't budge, squeeze or press on the handle to release the brake. (Traveling by train with lots of luggage can only be compared to making frequent and unsuccessful attempts at suicide.)

- Don't be fooled by European train designations. "Direct" may only mean "direct to the next station." Ask the clerk for the fastest train to your destination that doesn't require a supplemental charge. On the board listing trains, **Dep** is an international abbreviation for **Departure**; **Arr** is an abbreviation for **Arrival.**

Aboard trains

- Check to make sure the specific car you get on is going to your destination. Trains are often split up en route!

- If you have to get up for any reason, leave something on the seat—a newspaper, magazine, inexpensive hat, or handmade sign that says "occupied."

- If you stretch out, be sure to take your shoes off. This will prevent encounters with the conductor.

- Think twice before renting a **couchette** (a bunk bed in a compartment). If you do rent one, the conductor will give you a sheet (something between a hospital gown and a shroud), a blanket, and (if you beg) a pillow. The compartment will be noisy; and it will be either too hot or too cold. Whether your luggage remains outside or goes with you in the compartment, it will be vulnerable to thieves while you sleep.

Getting off trains

- Never get off a train until you've reached your final destination, unless you're sure the train will be in the station for a specific time.

- Never throw a ticket away until you've passed through the exit gates in the train station at your destination. Get information on the train you'll be taking next before you leave the station. If you find out this information right away, you won't have to return to or call the train station later.

- To save on washroom fees, always find a nearby restaurant if you need a toilet. Get a light snack and go to the bathroom there.

Trans Europe Express (TEE) Routes

Each Trans Europe Express (TEE) route has been given a name (see p. 50 for reservation information on TEEs). The following list includes some of the most popular trains.

Train	Route and time
Adriatico	Milan-Bari in 9 hours
Ambrosiano	Milan-Rome in 6 hours
Aquitane	Paris-Bordeaux in 4 hours
Arbalette	Paris-Zurich in 6 hours
Blauer Enzian	Hamburg-Munich-Klagenfurt in 13 hours
Brabant	Brussels-Paris in 2½ hours
Capitole du Matin	Paris-Toulouse in 6 hours
Capitole du Soir	Paris-Toulouse in 6 hours
Catalan	Geneva-Barcelona in 9 hours
Cisalpin	Paris-Milan-Venice in 11 hours
Edelweiss	Brussels-Zurich in 7 hours
Erasmus	Den Haag-Munich in 9 hours
Étendard	Paris-Bordeaux in 4 hours
Étoile du Nord	Amsterdam-Paris in 5 hours
Gottardo	Basel-Milan-Genoa in 8½ hours
Helvetia	Hamburg-Zurich in 9½ hours
Île de France	Amsterdam-Paris in 5 hours
Iris	Brussels-Zurich in 7 hours
Kleber	Paris-Strasbourg in 4 hours
Lemano	Geneva-Milan in 4 hours
Ligure	Milan-Avignon in 7½ hours
Mediolanum	Munich-Milan in 7 hours
Memling	Brussels-Paris in 2½ hours
Mistral	Paris-Nice in 9 hours
Molière	Paris-Cologne in 5 hours
Oiseau Bleu	Brussels-Paris in 3 hours
Parsifal	Hamburg-Cologne-Paris in 8 hours
Prinz Eugen	Hannover-Cologne-Vienna in 13 hours
Rembrandt	Amsterdam-Munich in 9 hours
Rheingold	Amsterdam-Geneva in 11 hours
Rhodanien	Paris-Marseilles in 6½ hours
Roland	Bremen-Milan in 13 hours
Rubens	Brussels-Paris in 2½ hours
Saphir	Brussels-Frankfurt-Nurnberg in 7½ hours
Settebello	Milan-Rome in 5½ hours
Stanislas	Paris-Strasbourg in 4 hours
Van Beethoven	Varying schedule between Amsterdam-Cologne-Nurnberg-Frankfurt
Vesuvio	Milan-Naples in 7½ hours

HITCHHIKING

Hitchhiking in Europe is far safer than the alarmists would have us believe; and many dangers can be avoided by traveling in pairs. It's illegal on superhighways—but that's where you get the long rides. So be prepared for occasional exchanges with the police. Keep them friendly by being polite and not arguing with them.

Prearranged rides

- Try to arrange rides before you even hit the road. Look for notices at the American Express office to see whether anyone is heading in the right direction. Check the bulletin boards at student halls and other youth-oriented places.

- Post your own notice, telling where you want to go. Make it easy to read and eye-catching—if it's funny, all the better. Use color to make it stand out. Be sure to tell people reading the notice how to contact you.

- Be willing to share gas costs with the drivers. It will still be less expensive than a train fare.

Where to hitch

- Use public transportation to reach the outskirts of a town and stand by a stop light or stop sign. Don't bother trying to get rides from a city center to the outskirts, since Europeans rarely pick up short-haulers —except for women hitching alone.

- Try standing near gas stations, rest stops, restaurants, and ferries.

- Don't hitch where there are truly inexpensive alternatives (as in Spain) or where it's generally disliked (as in southern France).

Before you hitch

- Make sure you have a map with you so you will be familiar with towns en route to your final destination.

- Make big, easy-to-read signs. Write down your destination, and the name of the next major town from where you are waiting, in order to pick up either long or short rides.

- Write the name of your destination in the appropriate European spelling: Athens (Athinia), Belgrade (Beograd), Brussels (Bruxelles), Copenhagen (København), Florence (Firenze), Geneva (Genève), Lisbon (Lisboa), Munich (Munchen), Naples (Napoli), Rome (Roma), Venice (Venezia), Vienna (Wien), and so on.

- If there is room on the sign, include the word **please:** **s.v.p.** (French), **bitte** (German), **per favore** (Italian), **faz favor** (Portuguese), **por favor** (Spanish).

- Put an American (or any other) flag on your pack. You don't have to be liked; you do have to be noticed.

- Stay as clean as possible. If your clothes are not fresh, splash on some cologne.

How to hitch

- Try to be either the first or the last person in a line of hitchhikers.

- Carry as little gear as possible and place what you've got behind you. Motorists don't like to pick up people who are carrying a lot of baggage.

- Take off your glasses (or your sunglasses) and hold your sign in front of you. Face the traffic. Extend your arm, your open palm toward the oncoming cars, your thumb up.

- If you can get someone to stop and talk to you, you've got a ride. Be polite but assertive.

- When you arrive in any large city, ask the driver to let you off near a tourist office or central train station (for easy access to information and room-finding services).

Hitchhikers' Success Rates

In hitchhiking, it's not who you are, but who is along with you, that determines how quickly you will get a ride.

Combination	Results
One woman	Immediate success.
Two women	Quick success.
One woman, one man	Short wait.
Three women	Slightly longer wait.
One man	Long wait.
Two men	Long, long wait.
Three men	Join the army.

Cautions for hitchhikers

- Stay away from curves. Place yourself on a straight stretch of road.

- Stop only in areas with good shoulders.
- If you are hitching after dark, wear something light-colored. Stand under a reflecting sign.
- Get well off the road to sleep or eat.
- If you notice that someone is a poor driver, ask to get out right away. No ride is worth a collision.
- Travel with a companion: the ideal team is a man and a woman. You'll avoid robbery and rape this way.

When to hit the road

- Sunrise is great, sunset is almost as good, and night-time is good but dangerous.
- Midday, particularly in the south, is awful, as are weekends, particularly Sundays in religious areas. Holidays are a bust.

Etiquette for hitchhikers

- The people already waiting at a hitchhiking area have the priority in choosing a spot, such as the front or back of a line of hitchhikers.
- If a car stops at the middle of a line of hitchers, it's every person for himself or herself. Generally, the person closest to the car will get the ride.
- You should entertain the driver, not go to sleep or sit silent. But don't demand attention—be sensitive to the driver's interest in conversation.

Vagabond lodging

Wily vagabonds on a budget soon learn that there are soft-water showers in many beach areas where you can wash off a week's grime for nothing. In cities, the favorite spots to sleep out are parks, church grounds (including cemeteries), and train stations. Youth hostels have been created with hitchhikers and bikers in mind (see p. 108); campgrounds offer showers, food, and safety for very little money (see p. 109).

- If you try sacking out on a beach, be as inconspicuous as possible. They're often patrolled.
- If you don't mind noise, ask permission from gas station attendants to sleep on any available grass. Most stations sell snacks, and you can use the washroom.
- If you sleep out, put all your valuables down in the bottom of your sleeping bag, not in your knapsack.

TAKING PUBLIC TRANSPORTATION AND TAXIS

The easiest way to learn about the ins and outs of public transportation is to ask the concierge or someone who speaks English at the hotel to explain it to you.

You can also easily ask the help of many people on the street in Austria (with some problems), Denmark, Finland, Germany (with some problems), Gibraltar, Great Britain, Iceland, Ireland, Malta, Netherlands, Norway, Sweden, and Switzerland (with some problems). In other countries, you may have frequent problems communicating. When you do, go to the nearest large hotel and ask the person at the front desk for help. Just remember that people usually like to help other people.

Public transit questions

- What is the best way to get from A to B?
- What is the least expensive way?
- Where do you get tickets or tokens? How much are they?
- Can I get a reduction for buying a pass or a set number of tickets?
- How do I get on to the bus or tram? (You must board some vehicles from the back.)

Public transit bargains

- **Amsterdam:** packets of tram tickets at discount prices, available at cigarette shops displaying Amsterdam Transportation Company emblems.
- **London:** "Go As You Please" tickets, at the Travel Enquiry Office at Piccadilly Circus.
- **Munich:** One-day **Turistenkarten,** at the Central Railway Station.
- **Paris:** booklet or **carnet** of ten tickets, at subway (**métro**) ticket windows.
- **Rome:** week pass at Central Station.
- **Stockholm:** three-day pass, at the tourist office.

Public transit tours

By using public transportation, you can often make tours at a fraction of the cost of organized tours.

- **Amsterdam:** pay for circular tours from and back to the Central Railway Station.

- **Helsinki**: public tourist tours cost a pittance.
- **London**: take bus No. 15 from Selfridges or on Oxford Street with panel marked "Aldgate"; or take No. 11 east from Victoria with panel marked "Liverpool Street."
- **Rome**: take bus No. 30 from Central Railway Station.
- **Paris**: the **bâteaux-mouches** on the Seine cost less in the morning.

The subway in Paris

In Paris, the best way to get around is to take the subway (**métro**). It will take you quickly and inexpensively to all major attractions.

- If you get lost on the **métro**, go to the nearest mechanical map and press the button for your destination. The whole route will light up. The name of the route is in bold print. You might have to move from one subway line to another to go all the way.

- Be careful not to go through the wrong gate when you get off a subway. There are two kinds of doors: one for connections ("**correspondance**") and one for street exits ("**sortie**"). If you take the wrong gate, you will have to pay another fare.

Taxis

In all but a few countries, such as Spain, Greece, and Portugal, taxis are extremely expensive. Try to avoid them by taking advantage of inexpensive, very good public transportation, including subways, buses, and trams.

- If you have to take a taxi, find out the approximate cost of the trip ahead of time by asking the information desk or at the front desk in a hotel, or by asking the cab driver himself. Find out also if there are minimum charges—perhaps the walk will be worth it.

- Be wary of asking a hotel to call you a cab, especially if you're staying in a more expensive hotel. Many of these establishments are served by special cabs—ones that offer extra comfort at an extra price. The less expensive cabs have already been warned to stay clear of such hotels, unless they are called by the hotel itself (a problem in Vienna). Insist on an ordinary metered cab!

- Always try to share the cost of a taxi with other people. This can be done easily on rides to major cities from outlying airports.

- Accept the fact that taxi rates go up late at night when

public transportation is not available.

• If you think a cab driver has swindled you, tell him that you're taking down the number of the cab and will report him to the central transportation authority or the police. If the driver has in fact duped you he'll probably lower the fare on the spot.

15
COMMUNICATING

The one consideration that most often discourages Americans from going to Europe in the first place is the "language barrier." Naturally, you can become better acquainted with Europeans if you can really speak their languages, but you can still have a great time in Europe with practically no foreign vocabulary. For one thing, you have sign-language fluency that you won't believe until you've tried it!

Another thing that concerns travelers is losing touch with the folks back home. In this age, though, you're as close as a phone to your family and friends, and mail delivery is quite reliable.

So relax—read this chapter—and enjoy!

SPEAKING

You'll have little trouble communicating in areas where there's heavy tourist traffic. You'll usually find someone in most hotels, restaurants, banks, shops, and travel terminals who can help you out. Only off the beaten path will you run into a language barrier, but even if you can't speak a word of a foreign language, you'll still get by.

Basic expressions

Since it takes years to learn a foreign language, most people don't even try. However, you should take the time to learn a few basic expressions and how to count to ten, not only because it will prove helpful but also because it's the right thing to do.

No book can show you how to pronounce foreign words correctly! Have a native speaker pronounce them for you (and don't be afraid to ask).

Asking directions

If you get lost, you may have a problem getting directions to your destination. In asking directions, the most important word is **to**.

- Open your mouth and say "ahh," as if you were in a dentist's chair. Follow "ahh" by the name of the place you're going: "ahh Paris," "ahh Trendelburg," and so on.

- If you'll point to a map as you do this, most Europeans will understand. Go ahead and use English in the rest of the sentence: for example, "I would like to go **ahh** Madrid."

Basic Expressions

English	French	Italian	Spanish	German	Portuguêse
Hello	bonjour	buon giorno	buenos dias	Guten Tag	bom dia
goodby	au revoir	arrivederci	adios	Auf Wiedersehn	adeus
slowly	lentement	lentamente	lentamente	langsam	lentamente
please	s'il vous plaît	per piacere	por favor	bitte	faz (faça) favor
thank you	merci	grazie	gracias	danke	obrigado (obrigada)
how much	combien	quanto	cuanto	wieviel	quanto
yes	oui	si	si	ja	sim
no	non	no	no	nein	não
I don't understand	je ne comprends pas	non capisco	no entiendo	Ich verstehe nicht	não entendo
how are you	comment allez-vous	come sta	como esta	wie geht es Ihnen	como esta
how do you say "____" in English	comment dit-on "____" en français	come si dice "____" in italiano	como se dice "____" en espanol	wie sagt man "____" auf Deutsch	como se diz "____" em por-tuguês

Numbers

English	French	Italian	Spanish	German	Portuguêse
one	un	uno	uno	eins	um
two	deux	due	dos	zwei	dois
three	trois	tre	tres	drei	tres
four	quatre	quattro	cuatro	vier	quatro
five	cinq	cinque	cinco	fünf	cinco
six	six	sei	seis	sechs	seis
seven	sept	sette	siete	sieben	sete
eight	huit	otto	ocho	acht	oito
nine	neuf	nove	nueve	neun	nove
ten	dix	dieci	diez	zehn	dez

- Remember that many cities are spelled differently in foreign languages. If someone doesn't understand you, maybe it's because you're not speaking his or her language! What good does it do to ask for Venice in Italy, when Italians call the city Venezia? Here are the major cities in their correct foreign spellings.

Athens	Athinai	**Lisbon**	Lisboa
Belgrade	Beograd	**Munich**	München
Brussels	Bruxelles	**Naples**	Napoli
Copenhagen	København	**Rome**	Roma
Florence	Firenze	**Venice**	Venezia
Geneva	Genève	**Vienna**	Wien

Tricks for communicating

- If someone doesn't understand you, repeat the statement—slowly, and without raising your voice. If he or she still doesn't understand, just smile and say thanks in the foreign language.

- If your vocabulary is limited, try to communicate in writing. Carry paper and a pen, and get waiters and clerks to write down prices for you.

- Drop your inhibitions and give sign language a try!

- In short, don't be intimidated by the language barrier. Don't let it stop you from venturing into remote areas that have been barely touched by modern tourism.

WRITING

Letters from home, and the postcards you send, can be especially important while you're traveling. No news may be good news, but news is still fun when you're far from home.

Staying in touch

- Duplicate your itinerary to give to friends and relatives you'd like to keep in touch with. Airlines sometimes can reach travelers for urgent messages if they have information on flight plans. But don't count on it!

- Ask correspondents to write "Hold for arrival" followed by the approximate date you'll be arriving, on all mail they send to hotels.

- Ask friends to **type**, not write, the address on the envelope. A typed address increases the odds that you'll get your mail!

- Ask them to address each envelope to an individual

person, not to a couple. Otherwise, the couple may have to show up to collect it.

- Tell people to send all letters airmail and to allow a week for delivery. Surface mail reaches Europe in six to eight weeks.

Alternative mail drops

If you have an exact itinerary but don't know where you'll find lodging, you can choose either of the following methods of receiving your mail abroad.

- Have the mail sent in care of American Express in the cities you'll be visiting. With either a credit card or some of their traveler's checks, this service is free. Expect long mail lines in the peak season at these offices. Your mail will be returned to sender after thirty days. Note that for a charge you can have mail forwarded from any American Express office.

- Have mail sent to General Delivery: **Poste restante** (French), **postlagernde Sendungen** (German), **Posta restante** (Italian), **Fermo posta** (Spanish), **posta-restante** (Portuguese). There's usually a small charge at General Delivery. And letters will be sent back after ten days. But the lines are usually short in comparison with those at the American Express office.

Sending mail home

- Stamps are sold at tobacco and stationery shops and in most hotels.

- Aerograms are the least expensive way to write letters to the U.S. You can buy these at the post office.

- Postcards are nearly as expensive to mail as letters, but are fun for the folks back home to receive.

- You'll often find inexpensive postcards in department stores and at street stands. They are cheaper than the ones found in hotels and are just as nice.

- Note that most hotels provide free envelopes and stationery. If you find none in your room, just ask.

PHONING AND CABLING

The telephone can do so much for you as you travel—help you book rooms and seats, hunt bargains and compare prices, and of course let you talk to people long distances away. European phone systems are sometimes idiosyncratic, but you can make good use of them with a few hints.

Local calls

The simplest places to make local calls are the hotel or the post office, where operators can help handle your calls.

- If you make local calls in a hotel, check on possible surcharges ahead of time. You can also use public pay phones, as in the U.S.

- There are no such surcharges at central post offices. You pay only for the call. Payment is often based on time alone.

- Note that many public phones require tokens, which you can buy in tobacco shops, post offices, bars, newsstands, and wherever public telephones exist.

- Note that in some areas you deposit coins or tokens **after** your party answers—and in some cases, you keep dropping them in throughout the call!

- If you have trouble locating a name in a foreign telephone book, ask for help. Note that some alphabets have extra letters, such as å, aa, ö, ø, and ò, which come at the end of Scandinavian alphabets.

Long distance calls from hotels

Many hotels add their own charges to long distance calls made from their rooms. In recent years, these charges have sometimes been three times the cost of the call—and the practice has sent warning ripples through the tourist industry.

Ireland, Israel, Portugal, and the Trust Houses Forte hotel chain in Great Britain belong to Teleplan, a system organized to reduce hotel surcharges. Perhaps other countries will join their efforts with similar programs.

- Never, never make a long distance call from a hotel room without checking on the hotel surcharge first.

- Note that U.S. telephone credit cards are accepted in many European countries and cut the cost of surcharges.

- If you don't have a telephone credit card, call collect. The overall rate for a collect call is quite high, but surcharges are lower. **Collect** in five languages: **P.C.V.** (French), **R-Gespräch** (German), **pagamento a carico del destinatario** (Italian), **à cobrar** (Portuguese), **pago revertido** (Spanish).

Avoiding hotel surcharges on calls

- Avoid surcharges of any kind by making long distance phone calls from the main telephone terminals in central post offices and in some railway stations and airports. The operator will tell you how long you should expect to wait to get a connection: times vary from a minute to several hours.

- Since these main telephone terminals can be packed in peak hours, avoid the crowds by going at unusual hours. Remember that it's many hours earlier in the day in the U.S.

- You'll be asked to write down your name, address, and telephone number; then the number, full name, and address of the person you're calling.

- You can call person to person, as in the States, but it's more expensive. **Person to person** in five languages: **prèavis** (French), **Foranmeldung** (German), **personale** (Italian), **persona a persona** (Spanish and Portuguese).

- If you can dial directly to the U.S. from your hotel room, play the "call back" game. Dial your friend, give him the number of your hotel and your room number, and ask him or her to call you back immediately. Since you pay only for the actual length of a call in Europe, your charge should be for a minute or less. Even if the hotel adds a surcharge of 100 percent or more, the total shouldn't break your bank.

Cables

A cable often costs as much as or more than a telephone call. It's paid for on a total word basis, which includes the name and address of the person to whom you're sending it. You can send a cable from central post offices in most major cities.

- Compare costs before you cable someone. A phone call may turn out to be more economical than you had expected.

16

DOING THINGS

This section is devoted to special-interest activities. You'll find information on shopping; sightseeing, the arts and nightlife; sex; photography; skiing and other outdoor sports—including tennis, golf, birdwatching, hunting, fishing, cycling, gliding, and nude bathing; and foreign study and work.

SHOPPING

You may be one of those people who enjoys shopping, who loves every minute spent in fashionable stores, street markets, and typical boutiques. If so, you will find Europe a delight.

Bargain hunting abroad

- Since most articles you can buy in Europe are also for sale in the U.S., study American prices before going abroad. Unless you do this, you will not know whether you're really getting a bargain.

- Unless a European item is much lower in price or of much higher quality than you can get in the U.S., don't buy it. You'll lose on the currency exchange, you'll have to lug or mail it home, and you may even have to pay duty on it. If you can't make a saving of 40 to 50 percent as compared to the U.S. price, don't buy!

- Shop around before you decide to buy something in Europe. By checking out several stores, you'll save many dollars.

- Ask what each shop's exchange rate is right away. If the rate is better in a bank, pay in local currency.

- Never buy American items abroad (this applies to everything!). Domestic brands are just as good.

- Never buy items in shops catering to crowds of tourists. Such items will always be sold at inflated prices.

- You can find superb bargains by settling for goods that have barely visible flaws, particularly in the case of porcelain and glass products.

- Always say "hello" and "goodby" to shopkeepers, even if you don't purchase anything in the store. This is basic courtesy in Europe.

Good Buy Guide to the Best in European Goods

The following chart will help you come up with some good buys in Europe, including articles typical of the area in which you're traveling. Most of the good buys included in this chart will be less expensive in Europe than in the U.S.

When in this country	Buy these items
Andorra	Excellent buys in cameras, crystal, dolls, leather, porcelain, stamps, watches, and wood products.
Austria	Antiques, art, Austrian jade, ceramics, costume jewelry, crèches, enamelware, fashions, figurines, guns, handbags (petit point), handmade blouses, knitwear, lace, leather, lingerie, porcelain (**Wiener Augarten**), ski wear, wood carvings, wrought iron.
Azores	Local handicrafts.
Belgium	Antiques, ceramics, chocolate, copperware, crystal, diamonds, glass, handmade shotguns, lace, leather, linen, paintings, pewter, silverware, wrought iron.
Canaries	Local handicrafts, liquor.
Denmark	Ceramics, china, food products, furniture, furs, Georg Jensen silver, glass, linen, pewter, Royal Copenhagen porcelain, teakwood, toys, watches.
Finland	Brass, ceramics, crystal, glass, jewelry, leather, pewter, wood products.
France	Alençon lace, antiques, Daum crystal, fashions, gloves, Lalique glass, leather, lingerie, paintings, perfume, scarves.
Germany	Beer steins, binoculars, cameras, comforters (down-filled), cuckoo clocks, cutlery, leather, music boxes, pewter, Rosenthal porcelain, toys, watches, wool products, wood carvings.
Gibraltar	Cameras, crystal, luxury items, perfume, tobacco.
Great Britain	Antique jewelry, antiques, books, cashmere, china, fabrics, glass, mod clothes, pewter, pipes, shoes, silk, suits, tobacco, tweeds, Wedgwood china, woolens.
Greece	Antiques, crocks, embroidered blouses, furs, leather, olivewood candlesticks, patterned coats, pottery, rugs, tote bags, silver jewelry, skins, wood carvings.
Iceland	Ceramics, pony skins, sheepskins, silver filigree, whalebone items, wool sweaters.
Ireland	Antiques, china, crystal, knitwear, lace, linen, rugs, silver, tweeds, whiskey.
Italy	Glass, gloves, gold jewelry, high fashion, leather (Florence), prints, shoes, silk, silver jewelry, straw goods.

(continued)

Luxembourg	Ceramics, crystal, jewelry, lace, linen.
Madeira	Lace, local handicrafts, Madeira wine.
Malta	Baskets, brass, ceramics, copper, dolls, embroidery, filigree, lace, perfume, pipes, pottery, wrought iron.
Majorca	Leather goods, Majorcan pearls.
Monaco	Dolls, jewelry, perfume.
Netherlands	Antiques, blankets, books, cheese, china, crystal (Leerdam), Delft porcelain, diamonds, figurines, gin (**genever**) in stone bottles, Oriental rugs, pewter, pipes, posters, prints, silver, tobacco.
Norway	Ceramics, glassware, pewter, sealskin boots, silver, ski wear, sweaters, Swiss watches, wooden salad bowls.
Portugal	Azulejo tiles, book covers, china, clay roosters, copper, cork, embroidery, filigree, furniture reproductions, guitars, handicrafts, lace, pewter, Port wine, pottery, rugs, Vista Alegre porcelain, wrought iron.
Scotland	Cutlery, Scotch, silver jewelry, sweaters, tweeds.
Spain	Gloves, high-fashion clothes, jewelry, lace, leather (Barcelona), mantillas, pottery, saffron, Talevera porcelain.
Sweden	Cutlery, handicrafts, Hasselblad cameras, modern furniture, Orrefors glass, pottery, silver jewelry, suede, steel products.
Switzerland	Cameras, cheese, chocolate, cuckoo clocks, embroidery, fondue sets, lace, music boxes, ski gear, steel products, toys, watches.
Yugoslavia	Copper, embroidery, filigree, lace, leather, rugs, wood carvings, wrought iron.

Duty-free shops

- Avoid most duty-free shops in airports and train stations, as they are now classic rip-off establishments. Prices there are often higher than comparable prices in quality stores.

- You can pick up truly duty-free goods on all international ships and ferries. Everyone else also knows this, which means that the lines will be long.

- Be sure to get in the right line, if you shop in a duty-free store on a ship or ferry. There's one line for liquor, another for cigarettes, and so on.

- Try to get in line early or late in the voyage. Otherwise, you'll wait an hour to pick up your bottle of cognac.

BARGAINING

It's actually improper for you to pay the asking price for goods in Spain, Portugal, Greece, and on most islands. It's equally improper in almost every European country, when you shop at open markets, small owner-operated shops, antique shops, art galleries, and flea markets.

Bargaining is not only accepted in these settings, it is also expected. If you're not used to bargaining, here's a chance to learn how.

Basic bargaining

Bargaining is an attitude, a position, a style. The attitude is wariness; the position is: "I won't buy unless it's a fair price." The style is tough but breezy, with a good sense of humor.

- Take your time and comparison shop first. When you've decided on what you really want, begin the bargaining game. Frivolous bargaining is unfair and a waste of the merchant's time.

- Ask for the price. Propose your own, undercutting the stated price by whatever you think you can get away with.

- State the U.S. cost in fair and accurate terms. Tell the merchant that you have no intention of buying unless you can make a substantial saving—of at least 40 to 50 percent. Shopkeepers respect this simple, honest approach to buying.

- State that you'll have to shop around because you want to come up with the best price in town and are willing to spend the time to do it. Prices will often slide down on the spot!

- Let a missing person play the bad guy. "Oh, I think it's beautiful. But my husband (wife) would be very upset if I spent that much."

- Be complimentary but shrewd, saying, "It's one of the finest pieces I've seen, but I really think it's overpriced."

- Evoke the expert. "I've got someone who really knows about these things. I'd better ask his advice before I spend all that much."

- Find a flaw. Almost everything has one, especially high-quality, handmade articles. I don't like this approach myself, but it does work. Try it only as a desperation ploy.

Advanced bargaining

- Play the add-on game. "I'll pay your price if you'll throw this extra item in." That so-called extra item may be exactly what you were after in the first place!

- Play the lump sum game. "I'll pay you this much for this, that, and that." You play the lump sum game after finding out the prices for the individual items. Naturally, you shave off a fair percentage for buying them as a group.

- If the price doesn't come down to what you're willing to pay, thank the merchant and be on your way. You'll be surprised how quickly this brings on a new round of negotiating. You'll sometimes be a block down the street before it starts!

Luxury shop bargaining

Polite bargaining is very effective in places where you don't want to be too aggressive. Don't let anybody tell you that it doesn't work! It does work, even in so-called luxury shops where you'd least expect it to. The following questions are all polite ways of asking, "How far will the price come down?"

- "Will the item soon be on sale?"

- "Is there a reduction for foreigners?"

- "Is there a discount for paying in traveler's checks?" This discount is quite common.

- "Are there professional discounts for writers (priests, teachers, doctors, lawyers, etc.)?" Become a professional for the moment if you think you can get away with it.

- "Is there a discount for cash purchases?" This is an implied threat to use a credit card.

Popular flea markets

- In Amsterdam head for Waterloopein on Saturday by taking the number 9 tram or the 5, 11, or 55 bus.

- In London, go to Bermondsey early Friday morning on the number 1 bus from Trafalgar Square (catch the bus by dawn). Also popular but not as good is the Portobello Market on Saturday, reached by bus number 15 on Oxford Street (panel marked Ladbroke Grove).

- In Madrid, try El Rastro, south of the Plaza Mayor along Ribera de Curtidores, on Sunday. Get there by taking a taxi to Plaza del Cascorro.

- In Paris, go to the Porte de Clignancourt on the subway line of the same name, or take the number 85 bus to rue des Rosiers, on Saturday, Sunday (best), and Monday.
- In Rome, it's the Porta Portese on Sunday. Take a taxi to get there.

SIGHTSEEING, THE ARTS, AND NIGHTLIFE

Tours of any city's famous sights are organized by local tour companies, large European tour companies, and tourist offices. But you can generally put together an equivalent tour for yourself, using the local bus or tram, for a fraction of the cost (see p. 161).

Most hotels and tourist offices offer free information on sightseeing and can give you maps that highlight the sights. They also have extensive information on how to use the local transportation network. When in doubt, just ask (see p. 161).

If you're a romantic, and want to try a buggy or gondola ride, expect to pay in spades, not hearts. Have the driver jot the price down on a piece of paper before you start.

Walking tours

Since you can only get to know a town intimately on foot, plan some time for walks—but take your physical condition into consideration as you plan.

- You can easily walk around the most interesting parts of these major cities: Amsterdam, Antwerp, Athens, Berlin, Bruges, Brussels (the center), Dublin, Edinburgh, Florence, Hamburg, Helsinki (with the tourist tram), Innsbruck, Lisbon, London (the center), Luxembourg City, Madrid (the center), Munich (with the tram), Oslo (with the tram), Salzburg, Stockholm, Toledo, Venice, and Vienna.

- You can walk much of Rome and Paris, although in these cities you'll need to use buses and subways to see all the major sights comfortably.

- Look for booklets, brochures, and special maps geared for walkers in the places you visit. Highly developed tourist areas may have do-it-yourself tours that follow routes past sights that are complete with explanatory plaques.

- Bring good, comfortable shoes for your walks.

- When your legs are tired, elevate them, keeping your knees slightly bent.

Zoos

The **Berlin** zoo, the game parks of **Great Britain,** and the deer park at Klampenborg six miles north of **Copenhagen** will be of interest to many tourists, particularly families traveling with children.

- For information on any of these contact the appropriate national tourist offices (see p. 23).

Museums and galleries

- Check ahead before making a special trip, since museums and galleries often close at odd times.

- Look for special flat-rate cards, good for admission to many places. At Alitalia Airline offices in the U.S., you can buy a card for a dollar that will get you into any state-owned museum in Italy for free. Look for similar bargains elsewhere.

- Note that students with student I.D.s (see p. 16) can often get reduced prices.

- Don't wear high heels to visit galleries and museums. Many forbid them because of the damage they do to floors. This is particularly true in France.

Theaters, movies, concerts, casinos

- You can often get into a London theater if you show up just before show time in person. This approach works best for singles.

- When an event or festival is solidly booked, try bribery. Go to the gate and slip the controller the equivalent of several dollars in foreign currency. "Well, maybe we could find a place for you."

- Arrive at foreign movies on time, because ticket takers may not let you in if you're late.

- To get into a casino, you may be asked to show your passport, and you may not be allowed in unless properly attired (i.e., sports coat and tie, or comparable dress for a woman).

SEX

Hardly a person goes to Europe without taking advantage of some of the most provocative aspects of the culture. After all, that's part of the fun, even on stodgy tours. Whether you choose to be a spectator or a participant, you should know that many cab drivers are paid kickbacks from clip joints to bring customers in. So if you ask a driver for information on sex or night life, you may be taken for a ride.

For women only

Women travelers have it made when it comes to finding companionship in Europe. Whether it's for a pleasant dinner companion or for a traveling partner, women will find it much easier than men will to meet members of the opposite sex.

- If you have a choice, consider taking a ship to Europe. Ocean voyages are wonderful settings for meeting excellent travelers. I can absolutely guarantee that you'll meet at least half a dozen attractive people if you take a ship to Europe.

- Tours also are a good source of companions. Your mutual destinations will highlight mutual interests.

- Train travel creates situations that encourage meeting new people. If you're game, make a point of being friendly to your fellow travelers—Europeans will wait for signals that you're interested in them.

- Younger women will find youth hostels, student tours, and similar youth-oriented places natural spots for meeting men. And each summer the American Express offices all over Europe become social headquarters to virtually six million Americans. They're an excellent source of impromptu traveling companions.

- Older women (as well as younger ones) will find that the lobbies, bars, and dining rooms of the finer hotels are good places to meet attractive, interesting men. Gigolos (men who may or may not be specifically paid for their company) collect in these areas. They can be delightful, but unscrupulous.

- Don't expect to meet local men as easily in northern Europe as you will in southern countries. Greece has perhaps the best prospects for meeting men. Italy is legendary.

- A word of caution: escort services and sleazy places are not worth your while (or money).

Directory of attractions

Sexy but classy shows The Raymond Revue Bar in **London** and the Crazy Horse, Lido, and Folies Bergères in **Paris**. Take in a show at the Lido from the bar (get there by 9:30 p.m., order one drink, and make it last for the whole show—and it will still be expensive).

Live sex on stage Casa Rosso, Oudezijds Achterburgwal 98, **Amsterdam**; Eden, Espergaerde (tickets sold in hotels) near **Copenhagen**; and Picant, Kaptensgatan 17, **Malmö** (in Sweden, across from Copenhagen by ferry).

Discreet sex   For the upper class: Bayadera, Westeinde 18, **Amsterdam**; Badner Hof, Badenalle, **Berlin**; and the houses of **Paris**.

Street hookers   For the nondiscreet. There are three main areas that are safe and reasonable. There's **Amsterdam**, world-famous for its colorful red light district, with sex for sale on a straightforward bargaining basis. **Hamburg**, known for its tawdry Reeperbahn, is not quite so safe, but is reasonable. Of course, there is also **Paris**, whose reputation for the bars of Pigalle precedes her. You have to buy champagne first, then the girl.

London's clubs   Basically a very expensive proposition. You ask for an escort, to whom you pay an escort fee (fifteen dollars). She can't leave the club until you've consumed a minimum amount of booze (seventy-five to a hundred dollars). Once that's done, you can leave. You will then have to pay the piper (seventy-five to a hundred and fifty dollars). You can do better in **Amsterdam**, **Hamburg**, and **Paris** for one tenth the price.

Hotel hookers   Every hotel denies it, but almost every expensive hotel encourages it. Bartenders can often say who's got the numbers or who's who in the bar—for a tip. Single men are often approached directly in a hotel lobby.

Courtesans   The caviar of the trade. You don't meet them, they meet you—and only if they want to.

Houses of Paris			
Name	**Address**	**Phone**	**Comments**
Mme Claude	rue Louis-David ? Paris 16è	525-55?6	Tops with reference only
Chez Billy	rue Paul-Valéry ? Paris 16è	553-794?	Serves diplomats
Chez Mad	rue Desaix 3? Paris 15è	783-29?7	Mainly for people in the entertainment business
Les Maronniers	rue de Chazelles 2? Paris 17è	924-281?	Couples only for swinging
La Villa Montespan	Avenue Montespan 1? Paris 16è	727-89??	Politicians take the plunge here

PHOTOGRAPHY

Europe offers a visual feast to photographers. Be sure you

bring enough film to record it! (I'm assuming that you have a thirty-five-millimeter camera; if you have some other type, some of these tips won't apply to your outfit.)

Equipment

- Be familiar with the workings of your equipment before you go abroad.
- Change all batteries and carry a few spares.
- Equip each lens with a Skylight or ultraviolet filter. Leave the filter on at all times (not only to improve photos but to protect the lens).
- Bring photographic lens tissue to clean lenses.

Film

- Avoid any film with "Professional" printed on the label. These require refrigeration!
- Specify either slide or print film. Slide film allows you to view every negative before deciding which ones you want made into prints—a real savings.
- Figure on a thirty-six-exposure roll for each day of travel abroad—at the minimum.
- Get films with different ASAs. ASA is a measurement of light sensitivity. You can then use the appropriate film for specific light conditions.
- Buy film that includes processing in its price. Since processing costs vary widely, do some comparison shopping in stores in your area and check out offers in photography magazines.
- As you finish each film, drop it in a prepaid mailer and send it back for processing. Be sure to write your U.S. address on the package! Send it to Kodak Processing Laboratories, 1712 South Prairie Avenue, Chicago, IL 60616.
- For information about processing abroad, get this pamphlet from Kodak: "International Photographic Headquarters" (No. XAC-16).

Security inspections

- The x-ray machines at airports can do damage to unexposed or undeveloped film, particularly those with ASAs over 400. Moreover, the effect is cumulative, so don't let the film go through these machines.
- Don't put film in luggage, which can be subjected to

high-level radiation. Carry it aboard the plane with you.

• Ask politely to have a visual inspection at check points.

Protecting camera gear

• If you put them in a plain carry-on bag, potential thieves won't suspect you're carrying valuable cameras.

• Always zip up the bag—even if you're nearby. Leave nothing exposed to chance and sticky fingers.

• Hand carry all cameras onto a plane. Cameras in your luggage could be lost with your luggage, taken out of your luggage, subjected to radiation, jostled about, or smashed.

• Never, never, **never** leave anything valuable on a plane during a stopover, no matter what the stewardess may say.

• In crowded places, wear cameras over your shoulder rather than around your neck. A thief snatching at your camera can easily hurt your neck in his eagerness.

• Do not leave cameras in car trunks and glove compartments. Not only are they vulnerable to theft, but the heat of the closed compartment can fuse the film to the glides.

Photo techniques

• Review the printed sheet that comes with the film to get a good idea of its light sensitivity and appropriate camera settings.

• Note: the light at noon is too harsh, and shadows too stark, to yield the best pictures. You'll get better light in the early morning and in the late afternoon.

• If your main subject is light-colored and your background is dark, give the film more light. If the subject is dark and the background is bright, give the film less light.

• If you discover that you've set your camera at the wrong ASA, continue to shoot at that setting. Make a note of the ASA setting that you used and attach it to the film container. Tell the processors about the mistake; they'll compensate for it in the processing.

Photo-taking etiquette

• Wherever you see the symbol of a camera with a line drawn through it (as in Yugoslavia), photography is forbidden. Unless you want to spend three days answer-

ing questions in the local police station, don't ta
photos in these areas. You'll encounter similar restri
tions in certain towns in Holland and at various historic
and religious sites as well. Observe them.

- In Moslem areas, you must be especially sensitive, since the Moslem religion discourages photography.

- Don't sneak photos, particularly of people. If you want to take someone's picture, be forthright and friendly—it will work wonders.

- Take someone along who speaks the language, if possible. If not, a smile rates second-best, but it's still good. Just lift the camera slowly, nod your head, and smile. If the person turns away or tosses his hand at you, don't take the photo. Or just say "please" (see p. 165) as you lift the camera, to get a reaction.

- Don't be afraid to pay for pictures. You can carry some small change for this purpose or plan to pay in a different way. Cigarettes will often cut the ice. Carry American brands, since the blond tobacco appeals to many foreigners as a change of pace and costs a cartload abroad.

- Other thank-you gifts: American coins (like Kennedy half-dollars); knickknacks, like pins or U.S. flags, medals, badges, and stamps (some people go gaga over the brightly colored ones.)

- If you work with a Polaroid or other instant camera, you can count on instant rapport with your subject.

- Don't gush or dawdle once you've taken a picture. Smile, shake hands, offer a gift—then go on about your business.

SKIING

Skiing is excellent in France, Germany, Italy, and Switzerland. If you intend to stay in a fashionable ski hotel, you must make reservations months in advance.

Ski packages

Many package deals are available that combine airfare, beds, meals, and lift tickets in one price. These are available from ski clubs, airlines, and specific tour operators specializing in skiing. Most tour packages are couple-oriented, with stiff charges for single supplements.

- If it's at all possible, go on a fourteen-day, rather than an eight-day, tour. You should allow yourself several days just to get used to altitude.

- To cut costs, try some of the lesser-known resorts in France and Italy, ski before February or after mid-March, and avoid the Christmas and Easter holidays.

Sources of information

- Always check snow conditions ahead of time before going to ski. For information, call (212) 757-6336 between December 15 and March 15.

- Get in touch with U.S. Ski Association, 1276 Champa Street, Denver, CO 80202 for information on ski clubs.

- Airlines with ski packages include Pan Am, TWA, Swissair, Air France, and Alitalia. If you live on the East Coast, fly Laker to London and hook on to a British ski package. For information, write University Travel, 44 Brattle Street, Cambridge, MA 02138; or British Caledonian Airway, 415 Madison Avenue, New York, NY 10017.

- Also contact Steve Lohr's Ski World, 3 East 54th Street, New York, NY 10022, 800-223-7606; (212) 751-3250.

- Consult the appropriate national tourist offices (see p. 23) as well, though their information is generally less helpful than the rest.

Lift tickets

- If the price of your lift ticket has not been included in the ski package, buy weekly passes only if you're an excellent and hard skier. Otherwise, buy coupons or point card tickets, which allow for several runs.

- If you do buy weekly passes, you'll need photomat photos to attach to the pass. Bring some from the U.S.

Clothes and boots

- Check on dress requirements with the tour operator or airline. Most ski resorts are quite informal, but a few are not.

- Lugging heavy boots is a chore, but it's worth it. Nothing is worse than the blisters caused by ill-fitting rental equipment.

OTHER OUTDOOR ACTIVITES

Skiing may well be the sport with the broadest appeal to most travelers. However, in this section you'll find helpful hints on other sports as well, even though some have limited followings.

Birdwatching

Birdwatching can be delightful throughout Europe. Here are

some of the prime spots you won't want to miss.

- Slimbridge, 12 miles west of Stroud in the Cotswolds of **Great Britain**. One of the finest wildfowl preserves in the world.

- Gannets at Eldey Rock, ducks on Lake Myvatn, pink-footed geese at Thjorsarver, and puffins on the Westmann Islands—by the thousands in **Iceland**. Remote and difficult trips for ardent bird lovers.

- The Camargue in southern **France** west of Marseilles, famed for its flamingos. Go in May.

- The Neusiedlersee lake east of Eisenstadt in **Austria**, best in late spring.

- The Las Marismas area of the Guadalquivir River in southern **Spain**, accessible by horseback and filled with ducks (mostly widgeon) in the fall.

- The flat coastal area of Zuidilijk Flevoland in the **Netherlands**.

Cycling

The tremendous popularity of the Tour de France gives you some idea of the reverence for cycling in **France**. Cycling is also highly recommended in **Belgium, Denmark, Germany** (the north), parts of **Italy, Luxembourg**, and the **Netherlands**.

- Read **Bicycle Touring in Europe**, by Karen and Gary Hawkins.

- Buy or rent a 10-speed bike (damage in transport and difficulties with repairs argue against bringing one from the U.S.). Rental is quite easy in Amsterdam and Copenhagen. Occasionally, a city such as Florence encourages the use of bikes and has a fleet available at low prices. Always contact the local tourist information offices abroad for advice.

- Remove the tire pump from the frame whenever you stop to eat, rest, or sleep. Many cyclists carry the pump in their gear to avoid being ripped off. Lock the bike routinely.

- Carry a tool kit and material for tire repairs. Reflective striping on you and the bike can help avoid accidents. Bring a flashlight since flats have a way of taking place at dusk.

- Don't overextend yourself. Until you're in shape, you should keep long distance riding to a minimum.

- Read the section on motorcycles for hints on recommended gear, including the best rain gear money can buy!

Fishing

Some of the best deep-sea fishing anywhere can be found off the **Canaries** near the coast of the Sahara. A limited number of charters is available in Gran Canaria. Excellent trout and salmon fishing can be found in **Iceland**, but the entire trip must be worked out in minute detail in advance. Be prepared to camp out or stay in modest hotels. The big advantage: many hours of daylight in the summer.

During mid-May, the mayflies hatch in **Ireland**, a country famed for its brown trout fishing.

Some of the finest trout and salmon rivers in the world are found in **Scotland**. Most stretches are privately owned, which means that a trip should be extremely well planned and well financed. Many hotels have their own fishing privileges. While it's generally very expensive, careful research can uncover reasonably priced daily licenses on some streams.

- Be sure to consult local guides or tackle shop clerks about local conditons and techniques.

- Pack along only your own most essential tackle, since local customs will probably dictate what you'll use. Rent or buy what's needed when you arrive.

Gliding

Gliders should head to **Great Britain** and **Germany**, both of which have centers for the sport.

- Both the British and German National Tourist Offices offer free pamphlets on gliding (see p. 23).

Golf

During the summer, you'll want to try the famous courses in **Scotland**. Enjoy golf in southern **Spain** and **Portugal** during the winter. Many courses are open at this time and are often associated with comfortable luxury hotels.

- If you belong to a private club in the U.S., bring a letter of introduction from the secretary as a way of breaking the ice at private Scottish clubs.

- If you stay in certain hotels, you'll have access to other private clubs as well.

Hiking

Of course, hiking is possible almost anywhere in the world, but it's a national pastime in Germany, Great Britain, and Switzerland.

- For information on hiking and available trails, contact the appropriate national tourist office (see p. 23) for free pamphlets and maps.

Hunting

Some of the best duck hunting in the world takes place near Valencia in southeastern **Spain**. Only a certain number of days are set aside for hunts, and blinds must be paid for and reserved months in advance. Very expensive and aristocratic!

Many Americans go to **Scotland** each fall to hunt grouse. Once again, this is an aristocratic pastime with arbitrary stays in ultra-expensive luxury hotels.

- You will hunt with double-barreled guns; no pumps are allowed.
- Bring formal evening attire.

Nude bathing

Europeans view this as a sport.

The Island of Sylt off **Denmark** turns into a nudists' mecca during the warmer months, as does St. Tropez in southern **France**. Also highly recommended are the islands off the coast of **Yugoslavia**.

- Bring sunscreening lotion if you're not a nudist ordinarily—for obvious applications.

STUDYING AND WORKING

What better ways are there of getting to know a country (and not incidentally, its language) than to live and learn with its people?

Foreign study

To enter a university abroad on equal footing with the rest of the students, you must already have completed two years of college in the U.S. However, you can take many courses (but none for credit) with only a high school diploma.

Courses abroad are considerably less expensive than in the U.S., because education has been subsidized by the government. But summer study, geared mainly to foreigners, is very expensive in comparison with the regular courses.

- Arrange for a student visa if you're planning long-term study. Contact the appropriate national tourist office (see p. 23) for help with visas and other information.

- Explore low-cost housing and meals for which students are eligible.

- Arrange to have your **school transcripts** (with imprinted seals); a **health certificate** signed by your doctor, which attests to your good health; and your **birth certificate** (or a notarized copy) translated.

- Get several extra passport photos.

Language courses

- Note: the finest French is spoken around Tours in central France; while the best Italian is heard in Tuscany, the region surrounding Florence.

- You can learn French cheaply in superb graduated French courses for foreigners in major university towns in France.

- You can learn German at the Goethe Institute, also set up for foreigners, in schools throughout Germany. But it's expensive.

- You can learn Italian and Spanish cheaply in less expensive courses for foreigners at universities in Italy and Spain, respectively.

Working abroad

All in all, it's not a bright picture for Americans seeking work in Europe. It's much easier to earn money in the U.S. Jobs abroad are scarce, and for long-term jobs abroad you'll need work permits, which are a hassle to get. However, lots of menial work is available illegally, for which you won't need a work permit!

- Women can readily get **au pair** jobs—a combination of light housework and babysitting. They pay practically nothing, but often include room and board.

- English teachers and tutors are often needed—at low wages.

- Athletes can sometimes get jobs for city teams if they're highly skilled and willing to work for a small wage and/or room and board.

17

STAYING HEALTHY

Certain health problems come up frequently when people travel, so frequently that they become standard jokes. However, for the person suffering the indignities of diarrhea, nothing seems amusing. These hints can prevent and cure some of the most common complaints that may appear in Europe.

HEALTH CARE ABROAD

Health care abroad can be excellent, but you have to know the ropes to take advantage of the good and to avoid the bad.

Doctors and drugs

- If you need a doctor for a minor illness, you can trust the concierge of any hotel to come up with the name of a doctor. If you feel that language will be a problem, you can get the names of English-speaking doctors from American consulates, motor clubs, Intermedic, and IAMAT (see pp. 14-15).

- If you can't find an American consulate, try a British one. Or call a representative of an American shipping company or airline. They can usually help.

- To find a pharmacy that's open all night, go to the nearest one. If it's closed, look on the door and you'll see the name and address of the place open that night.

Hospitals and clinics

- Avoid public hospitals if you are seriously ill. I've found European public hospitals to be inspired by Dante, going so far as to put a cast on a leg which didn't need one. And even that was done badly. Go to a **private clinic.**

GENERAL HEALTH PROBLEMS

Many discomforts or minor ailments that come with travel are easily prevented or cured.

Anxiety

It's very common for travelers to experience anxiety in Europe.

- Try to get plenty of rest, have a good meal with a beer or glass of wine, and take a tranquilizer, if absolutely necessary.

- Write a letter to a friend. It often soothes jangled nerves and allows you to unload some of your feelings.
- Do some shopping, even if you don't intend to buy anything.
- Don't feel compulsive about sightseeing and schedules!

Bee stings

The normal reaction to a bee sting is pain, swelling, and itching. A not-so-normal reaction to a sting produces hives, rash, swelling in the throat area, spasm, and even breathing problems. A severe reaction results in shock and dropping blood pressure, which can lead to death (see p. 195).

- Reduce pain with aspirin, reduce swelling with ice, and relieve itching with calamine lotion.
- No calamine lotion? Use toothpaste, not as good but passable.
- If you or someone else has a severe reaction, seek medical help immediately!
- If you plan extensive hiking, cycling, or bike riding through Europe, plan seriously for the possibility of bee stings.

Constipation

- Try to follow a routine and get plenty of exercise during the day. Walk whenever possible. Not only does it help the body, but it proves one of the most enjoyable ways of getting to know a town or city.
- Drink mineral water or mix bran into fruit juices as laxatives if this is a chronic problem. You can get bran at health food stores and carry a small packet with you.

Diabetes

- See p. 15 for the name of an organization that will give you helpful information.
- Carry urine-testing equipment, regular and long-lasting insulin, oral drugs or syringes, extra carbohydrates (schedules do get fouled up), and a doctor's note stating that you're diabetic for you to show to customs agents.
- Wear identification that states the nature of and treatment for your illness.
- If you buy insulin abroad, learn about the variations in strengths and how to deal with them before going to Europe.

- Order special meals ahead of time for plane trips.

Diarrhea: prevention

- One sure way to prevent diarrhea is to avoid possible sources of contaminated food and drink.

- Drink only tea, coffee, beer, wine, distilled liquor, bottled soft drinks, and **carbonated** bottled water (be sure the water is opened at your table). Noncarbonated bottled water may or may not be safe.

- Avoid tap water that hasn't been purified, even for brushing teeth. Ice for drinks is often made from tap water. Most problems with water occur in Italy, Portugal, and Spain.

- If you drink from a can or bottle, wipe off any moisture around the area from which you'll be drinking. Use straws if possible.

- You can purify water by adding Halazone tablets (fine if fresh, but they break down in time), by boiling it for ten minutes, or by adding five drops of 2 percent tincture of iodine to one quart of water and letting it stand for thirty minutes. If the water is cloudy, add ten drops. Alcohol will **not** purify water!

- You can also use liquid chlorine bleach. If it's a 1 percent solution, add ten drops per quart and let stand thirty minutes. If it's a 4 to 6 percent solution, add only two to four drops per quart. The water should have a slight odor of chlorine. If it doesn't, add a few more drops.

- If you want to play the odds, let the hot water run from the tap until it's scalding—then fill up a container and let it cool off.

- Stay away from foods sold by street vendors, never eat raw meat or fish (including shellfish), and avoid salads. Stick to fruits and vegetables that can be peeled.

- Stay away from milk or milk products unless you're sure they've been pasteurized. This includes local cheeses in rural areas!

- Avoid precooked foods that have been allowed to stand around for awhile.

- Pepto-Bismol may prevent diarrhea, according to a recent report. At least, it's said to cut down on the overall incidence of diarrhea with a dosage of four tablespoons per day.

Diarrhea: treatment

Diarrhea generally lasts for three to four days. If it goes on for more than five days, or if you notice blood in your stool, see a doctor.

- Lomotil works well, but should not be used for more than a day or two. It has the potential of locking in the infection.

- Drink clear liquids with salt and sugar added. To prevent dehydration, a pinch of salt in a bottle of cola is highly recommended.

- Avoid fatty, spicy foods and stick to bland foods until you're recovered.

- Experienced travelers who go into remote areas often carry a special preparation with them. Combine 1 teaspoon salt, ½ teaspoon baking soda, 4 teaspoons cream of tartar, and 6 teaspoons sugar. Add this to 1 quart of water. You can prepare the mixture ahead of time and pack it along—just in case you need it.

- Note: do not buy drugs for diarrhea abroad. Never buy **entero-vioform**. This preparation, which cannot even be sold in the U.S., is said to cause blindness and other complications.

Ear pain

- Clean out nasal passages and sinuses with spray before flying. Repeat fifteen to twenty minutes before landing.

- No spray? Chew gum, swallow, and yawn frequently.

Exhaustion

- Prevent exhaustion by breaking up marathon trips with frequent stopovers.

- Cure it by slowing down the pace and forcing yourself to nap occasionally.

Exposure to cold

- Eat more food; drink hot liquids.

- Exercise moderately to increase body temperature, and cover all exposed areas, especially the head, hands, and feet.

- If your hands get cold, shove them inside your clothing against your body.

- Remember never to rub cold and exposed skin and to thaw overly cold hands or feet in water only slightly warmer than skin temperature.

Exposure to heat

- Wear loose clothing, light in color and weight.

- Wear a hat and stay in the shade as much as possible.

- Try following the local custom of napping from noon to four in southern countries during the July and August heat.

- Drink lots of water with fresh lemon and lime juice, and make sure there's salt in your diet.

- Avoid alcohol and smoking—if it's humanly possible.

- Travel in desert areas at dawn or dusk.

Eye problems

- Bring spare eyeglasses in a hard case.

- Carry your lens prescription in your wallet.

- If a lens breaks, keep the bits. A lens can be duplicated from these pieces, even if you don't know your prescription.

- If you get a speck in your eye, pull the upper lid over the lower one, then let go. The irritant will often be dislodged.

- If that doesn't work, have someone else find the spot and gently touch it with a piece of tissue. It will usually adhere to the tissue and be lifted off the eye.

Feminine hygiene

- **Sanitary napkins** in five languages: **bandes hygiéniques** (French), **Damenbinden** (German), **compresa hygiénica** (Italian), **absorviente feminina** (Spanish), **absorvente feminina** (Portuguese).

- Tampons may only be available at pharmacies in some areas.

Food poisoning

- During the summer, avoid foods not properly refrigerated, including mayonnaise, custard-filled pastries, and shellfish. Food poisoning lasts about three days. Little can be done for this illness, which can only be described as the next worst thing to dying.

Hemorrhoids

- Bring medicine and Tucks, which contain witch hazel to relieve itching.

- Carry your own toilet paper. American brands are much softer than most paper available in Europe.

Insect bites

- Vinegar helps when nothing else is available.

Insomnia

- During the day, get plenty of exercise, drink lots of liquids, and eat a well-balanced diet high in protein.

- Drink small amounts of beer, which contains sleep-inducing lupulin (a product of hops).

- Take a warm bath and eat a light snack with milk just before going to bed. Milk contains L-tryptophan and calcium; both induce sleep.

- Keep your room dark and quiet. If your hotel is noisy, use earplugs. If the room is too light, use a mask.

- Set up a routine to induce drowsiness, such as reading before falling asleep. Follow this routine both at home and when you're on a trip, because it will trigger sleep.

- Things to avoid: too much alcohol; late-night meals, especially spicy ones; chocolate and cola, since both contain caffeine; and afternoon naps. Also try to avoid sleep-inducing drugs. Although they work, they also cause sleep disturbances and have other side effects that do more harm than good in the long run.

Jet lag
- See p. 87.

Motion sickness

- To avoid motion sickness, take over-the-counter drugs before the beginning of your trip. If you take them after motion sickness starts, they'll be useless.

- Before a long trip, eat a hearty breakfast. During the trip eat frequent, light snacks. Avoid alcohol.

- On a ship, try to get a cabin in the middle near the waterline. This will cut down on the overall rocking. On a plane, pick a seat in the center, over the wing area. In a car, place yourself up front, or even drive. Drivers rarely experience motion sickness, since they're concentrating on the road!

- If you feel nauseous, try to avoid the smell of food and tobacco; close your eyes or put on an eye mask; stay in a reclining position.

Sunburn

- Prevent sunburn with proper clothing and common sense, including the use of lotions and sunscreening agents. Ease pain with ointments or vinegar.

18

TROUBLESHOOTING

Even in the best-planned trips, something is bound to go awry. Here's hoping that you never have to refer to this section!

LOSSES

No one wants to think about losing something while planning an enjoyable trip, but losses occur with such regularity that you should be forewarned with the following tips.

Lost passports

- If you lose your passport in the U.S., report the loss immediately to the local branch of the Justice Department.

- If you lose your passport in Europe, contact the nearest American consulate.

- Report the loss to the local police. They will give you a receipt, which you can use as a temporary I.D. You must carry it with you at all times.

- Carry two spare passport photos, a notarized copy of your birth certificate, a photocopy of the information on pp. 2 and 3 of your passport, and a note listing your passport number to speed up the process of getting a new passport.

Lost traveler's checks and credit cards

- Report the loss immediately to the company, if you should lose your traveler's checks or credit cards. You're liable for fifty dollars at most for unauthorized use of any credit card, but if you report the loss before any unauthorized use takes place, you're not liable at all. Paying nothing is better than paying fifty bucks!

- Make a list of the numbers of your unused traveler's checks. Avis will refund up to one hundred dollars in American Express traveler's checks on weekends, holidays, and late nights if local American Express offices are closed (see p. 115).

Robberies

- If you are robbed, report it to the hotel or restaurant management. And also report it to the police. If you follow this procedure, you can get reimbursed by your insurance company. Ask for a copy of the report as proof of your goodwill.

- Prevent a robbery in the first place by following the hints on p. 117.

ACCIDENTS

Yes, accidents do happen. Even minor ones can cause serious disruption of your trip. Here's advice to smooth over the bumps.

Immediate actions

- If another car is involved, or if you cause serious damage to property, or if you hurt someone, you should stick to the spot like glue. Take photos if you can.

Summoning help

- Naturally, if someone is hurt, try to get hold of an ambulance or the police immediately. In rural areas, flag down an oncoming car and ask the driver to do it for you. Administer basic first aid when necessary by stopping bleeding, getting the person breathing, keeping the person warm to prevent shock. But don't move anybody who is hurt. Let the police or medics do that!

- If someone you know has been seriously hurt, try to have him admitted to a private clinic. You may want an English-speaking doctor (see p. 15). If the situation is critical, the nearest hospital will have to do, but public hospitals in some areas can offer cures that are worse than the original complaint.

After an accident

- Be prepared for lengthy questions and a detailed report. Note that these reports can be used in court. If you're at fault in a serious accident, you may be liable for a prison sentence.

- Expect trouble if you didn't have your passport with you. You may spend some time behind bars—even if the accident wasn't your fault.

- Contact your car insurance company. The insurance company will tell you what to do regarding repairs.

- If you own the car and intend to ship it back to the U.S., have all repairs done in the U.S. The reason: you can collect for the damage done to the car. You can claim a much lower value for it and pay a proportionately lower tax coming through customs.

Emergency Phone Numbers

This list of numbers might prove helpful in an emergency. Note that emergency numbers are often listed in the front of telephone books abroad, as they are in the U.S.

These numbers are to be used only in an emergency situation—not for such things as a flat tire or breakdown! They will not work everywhere—as in some rural areas—but they're better than no numbers at all.

Austria   133 (police), 144 (ambulance)

Belgium   900 or 901

Denmark   000

Finland   000

France   Local number of **Brigade de Gendarmerie**

Germany   110

Great Britain   999

Greece   100 or 109 (police), 525555 (ambulance)

Ireland   Local number of **Garda**

Italy   113

Luxembourg   012

Netherlands   222222 (in Amsterdam or The Hague),
                       94 (in Rotterdam), (03438) 4321
                       (anywhere else)

Norway   331290 (police), 201090 (ambulance)

Portugal   115

Spain   091 (in Madrid or Barcelona)

Sweden   90000

Switzerland   17, 117, or 11
                       12, 111, 112 (no money needed for call)

Yugoslavia   92 (police), 94 (ambulance)

ARRESTS

If you're in doubt about your legal rights, ask to speak to someone from the nearest American consulate. Note that your rights are defined by local law, not American law!

Drunken driving

If you get arrested for drunk driving, you may be in real trouble. In many countries, it will mean an automatic jail sentence of a month or more, for locals and foreigners alike.

- Note that the legal definition of drunkenness may apply after no more than a drink or two in Scandinavia and Austria. If your drunkenness causes an accident, you're open to criminal charges.

- Take a taxi if you've had too much to drink!

Minor traffic violations

If you're arrested for minor traffic violations, you will be asked to pay a fine (see pp. 150-51).

Drug violations

If you're arrested for smuggling drugs, you may well spend many years in a foreign jail. It may be tempting to bring hash from Morocco into Spain, but a six-year jail term is hardly worth the risk.

- Never carry illegal drugs, even small amounts, across a border!

Political violations

Some countries impose stiff fines and jail terms for any activity directed against the state or its political system. This would include insulting behavior and denigration of a national flag.

- Mind your manners—you are a guest.

DUTIES AND U.S. CUSTOMS

The brochure "Know Before You Go" gives detailed information on customs procedures. You can get it from U.S. Customs Service, P.O. Box 7118, Washington, DC 20044, or from any local customs office.

Duty regulations

- Products made in some developing countries can be imported free of any duty. For a list of the countries and exempt products, ask for "GSP and the Traveler," available free from U.S. Customs Service, Washington, DC 20229.

- You are now allowed to bring back free of duty goods

with a total retail value of $300. You pay only 10 percent duty on the next $600. After that, you pay varying duties, depending upon the nature of the imported article.

Customs inspections

- Be sure to have ready your registration slip for valuable articles that you took from the U.S. to Europe, or you'll have to pay duty on them if you're over the $300 limit (see p. 82).

- Have all your sales receipts at hand, to prove the actual cost of things purchased in Europe. Note that customs officials know relative retail values almost to the cent. You're not going to get by with a doctored sales receipt. Furthermore, the new allowances seem liberal and appropriate.

- Note that a customs official may ask you to empty your pockets, and very rarely will he (or she) check your body. If it makes you feel better, you're expected to be slightly nervous. But don't make jokes, jabber, or volunteer information. Answer all questions as politely and briefly as possible.

- Note also that U.S. Customs inspectors check baggage carefully for porno, plants, drugs, perfume, excess alcohol (you can bring back one quart), and excess cigarettes (you can bring back two hundred) and cigars (you can bring back one hundred).

Possible snags in customs

- If an official catches you bringing in something that you haven't declared, admit the mistake immediately. Just say that you forgot about it. Avoid confrontations and arguments.

- If an official breaks an item while searching bags, file a U.S. Government form SF9-5 with the regional customs office in the state where the damage takes place. You'll be reimbursed.

U.S. Customs regulations on packages shipped separately

- You can send any personal article home without paying duty, as long as it was purchased in the U.S. Mark the package "American goods returned."

- You can send a friend one duty-free gift every day just as long as its retail value is less than twenty-five dollars. Mark the package "Unsolicited gift (value less than $25)." Clearly state on the package what the gift is.

- You can also send many separate gifts in one large package, as long as each gift is individually wrapped and marked with the name of the recipient. The nature of every gift within the large package must be marked on the outside.

- You must pay duty on all items you send to your home, but not on those gifts sent to friends. Many travelers arrange to send items to friends, who will hold them for their return.

SHIPPING GOODS HOME

The safest and surest way of getting any article to your home is to carry it with you. The second-best way is to ship it home; the least sure way is to have a shop ship it.

In the nine Common Market countries and Austria, you'll pay 8 to 18 percent VAT (Value Added Tax) on all purchases unless they are sent out of the country. In short, you don't pay local taxes for packages shipped to the U.S.

Shipping goods through shops

You may want to oversee the wrapping of your purchase to make sure that the right item is packed and that it is properly protected (which it generally is).

- If you have a store ship your package for you, have the shipping date clearly marked on your bill of sale.

- Ask the clerk to note down the cost of any insurance, the value of the insurance, any shipping charges, and the mode of delivery.

- Specify airmail or surface mail. Airmail costs more, but is safer and faster. Surface mail may take months to arrive and increases the odds of damage.

Using brokers

Goods may come into the U.S. through a broker, who may or may not inform you of their arrival. Unless it's clearly understood that packages are to be delivered to your home address, they may simply sit in storage in some remote warehouse. Try to avoid using brokers whenever possible.

- Get the name and address of any middlemen.

- Be prepared to pay storage fees for any package that sits in the warehouse. If you want your goods, you will pay the charge.

Shipping goods on your own

- Check with the post office if you'll be mailing large or heavy packages. Size and weight limitations apply.

- If you find you have to send a package through a freight office, call several and compare costs and service before signing on the dotted line.

- Use twine instead of tape. Twine can be sealed with wax if you want to insure the package. In some countries, you will not be able to insure international mail.

- If you're sending books back, be sure to get the special book rate.

- Don't plan to send fragile items, since they will usually be broken in the mail—not because the package was poorly wrapped or mishandled, but because it was unwrapped in customs, only to be poorly rewrapped! Carry fragile items with you or skip buying them altogether. (If you do buy something fragile, try to arrange to pick it up at the end of the trip.)

APPENDIX

Climate Chart

This chart gives you a capsule picture of each country's weather, followed by a breakdown of its average temperature (in degrees Fahrenheit) and rainfall (in inches) on a month-to-month basis. Naturally, temperatures drop by ten degrees or so in the evening to rise again by ten degrees or so over the average at midday—so take these overall averages with a grain of salt. Nevertheless, the chart does provide a good, accurate idea of what to expect in the way of weather at any time—and might influence your decision as to when to make a trip to Europe.

Country		J	F	M	A	M	J	J	A	S	O	N	D
Andorra Almost all people go to Andorra in the summer, although late spring and early fall can be quite mild.	rain	1.5	1.5	1.5	1.5	3	2	2	2	1.5	2	2	1.5
	temp.	27	31	37	49	57	63	67	67	60	49	35	31
Austria Most mountain resorts are open in summer and winter only. Major cities tend to be shrouded in a gray mist during the winter, while both spring and fall can be pleasant in the valleys. Bring a raincoat.	rain	1.5	1.5	1.5	2	3	2.5	3.5	3	1.5	2	2	1.5
	temp.	29	33	40	51	58	64	68	66	60	50	40	34
Azores Very bleak in the off season. Try to go in the summer.	rain	5	4	4	2.5	2.5	1.5	1	1	3	4	5	4
	temp.	57	57	58	59	61	65	69	71	70	66	62	59
Belgium Off-season weather is poor in Belgium. Occasionally, you'll find mild weather in November, known as "St. Martin's Summer." March is one of the worst months. From April to mid-October you'll find the nicest weather, but it's unpredictable, so bring a raincoat!	rain	2.5	2	2	2.5	2	2	3	3	2	3	3	1.5
	temp	36	38	43	47	55	61	63	63	59	50	44	39
Canaries For these isolated islands off the North African coast, good weather is the main attraction. Temperature and rainfall vary from island to island. Lanzarote and Fuerteventura may go for months, sometimes years, without rain, whereas La Palma and Tenerife tend to be lush along the coast. Very mild even in midwinter.	rain	1.5	1.5	1	.5	0	0	0	0	0	0	2	2
	temp.	63	63	64	65	67	70	75	76	73	72	69	64

		J	F	M	A	M	J	J	A	S	O	N	D
Corsica	rain	3	2.5	2	2	2	1	.5	1	2	3.5	4	4
	temp.	45	47	51	54	61	67	71	71	71	61	52	47
Crete	rain	4	2	2	1	.5	0	0	0	.5	2	2.5	4
	temp.	53	54	56	62	69	75	79	79	75	69	62	56
Denmark	rain	2	1.5	1.5	1.5	.5	2	2	3	2.5	2	2	2
	temp.	32	32	35	43	53	60	63	62	57	48	42	36
Finland	rain	2	1.5	1	1.5	1.5	2	3	3	2.5	2.5	2.5	2
	temp.	20	19	24	35	48	57	62	60	51	40	33	27
France	rain	2	2	1.5	1.5	2	2	3	2	2	2	2	2
	temp.	36	38	44	50	57	62	66	65	61	52	44	39
Germany	rain	1.5	1.5	1	1.5	2	2.5	2.5	2	2	2	2	1.5
	temp.	29	32	39	48	57	63	66	65	59	47	40	34
Gibraltar	rain	6	4	5	2.5	1	0	0	0	.5	2.5	6	5
	temp.	52	55	57	61	66	70	75	75	72	67	61	57
Great Britain	rain	3.5	3	3	2.5	2	1.5	1	1	2	1	3	4.5
	temp.	38	40	43	47	51	53	61	60	53	51	43	43
Greece	rain	2.5	1.5	1.5	1	1	.5	.5	.5	.5	2	2	3
	temp.	48	50	32	59	68	76	81	80	74	66	58	52

Corsica Go in the summer. Too bleak in the off season.

Crete Warm and dry much of the year. Mild but not swimming weather in winter. Torrid summers.

Denmark Best visited from mid-May to mid-September, but bring a rain-coat.

Finland Best visited late May to early September.

France Whole country lovely from April to late October. North (including Paris) cold and damp during the winter season. Riviera mild in the off season, but not warm enough for swimming.

Germany Whole country lovely from April to late October. Munich very cold during the winter. Heavy snowfalls in the south and mountain areas, including the Black Forest.

Gibraltar Very hot during the summer, quite mild in winter.

Great Britain Nicest weather in June. Good weather much of the time from April to late October, although you'll need a good umbrella. Cold with occasional snows during the winter.

Greece Scorching hot weather from late May to early September. Mild in spring and fall, so-so in winter—OK for sightseeing but not for swimming. Very cold in the north at that time.

Country		J	F	M	A	M	J	J	A	S	O	N	D
Iceland Basically a summer-only island as far as tourism goes, because that's when the weather is best. Bring rain gear nevertheless.	rain	3.5	2.5	2.5	2	1.5	1.5	2	2.5	3	4	3.5	3.5
	temp.	32	32	34	37	44	49	52	49	47	41	36	34
Ireland Wet much of the time, even in the summer. Wet, penetrating cold in the winter.	rain	3	2	2	2	2.5	2	3	3	3	3	3	3
	temp.	40	41	43	46	51	56	59	59	55	50	44	42
Italy Excellent weather in most areas from April to late October. Very mild in the south during the winter, but not mild enough for enjoyable swimming—except in heated pools. Rome, Florence, and Venice can be stifling in the summer heat, and most Italians take a break from noon to 4:00 p.m.	rain	3.5	3	3	2	2	2	.5	.5	3	4.5	4.5	4
	temp.	46	48	52	56	63	70	76	75	70	62	54	49
Liechtenstein Same sort of weather as Austria.	rain	1.5	1.5	2	1.5	3	2.5	3.5	3	1.5	2	2	1.5
	temp.	29	33	40	51	58	64	68	66	60	50	40	34
Luxembourg Often damp and misty, even during the summer. Cold and drizzly in the off season.	rain	3	2	2	2	2.5	2.5	2.5	3	2.5	2	2.5	2.5
	temp.	32	34	41	47	55	60	62	62	57	48	40	34
Madeira Noted for its mild off-season weather. A favorite of the British at Christmas. At its best in spring (lush flowers) and fall (wine harvest).	rain	3.5	3.5	3	2	1	0	0	1	1	3	4	4
	temp.	60	60	61	61	63	66	70	71	70	69	65	61
Majorca Hot and bright sun during the summer, very mild even in winter—but not mild enough for ocean swimming.	rain	1.5	1.5	1.5	1	.5	.5	0	1	2.5	3	2.5	2
	temp.	50	51	53	58	62	70	75	76	72	64	57	52
Malta Dry, hot summers with mild winters—again, "mild" in the Mediterranean does not mean ideal for swimming.	rain	3.5	2	2	1.5	.5	0	0	0	1.5	6	4.5	3
	temp.	53	53	56	60	65	73	78	79	75	70	62	57
Menorca See Majorca.	rain	2.5	2	2	1.5	1	1	0	1	3	5.5	4	3
	temp.	50	51	53	57	59	70	75	75	71	64	57	53
Netherlands Best weather from mid-April to late October, with frequent showers. Cold in the off season: you'll need a warm coat.	rain	2.5	2	2	2	2	2	2	3	3	3	3	2.5
	temp.	34	35	41	47	53	60	62	62	57	50	43	37

		J	F	M	A	M	J	J	A	S	O	N	D
Norway	rain	2.5	1.5	1	1.5	1.5	3	3.5	4	3.5	3.5	2.5	2.5
	temp.	23	25	31	41	51	58	62	61	50	40	34	28
Portugal	rain	4.5	3	4	2	1.5	.5	0	0	1.5	2.5	3.5	4
	temp.	51	52	56	60	62	68	71	72	70	64	58	52
Sardinia	rain	2	1.5	1.5	1	1.5	.5	0	.5	1	3	2	2
	temp.	48	49	53	57	62	70	75	75	71	64	57	51
Sicily	rain	4	2	2.5	1.5	1	0	0	.5	1.5	5.5	4	3
	temp.	50	51	53	57	64	71	77	78	73	66	58	52
Spain	rain	1.5	1.5	2	2	2	1	.5	.5	1.5	2	2	2
	temp.	41	43	50	54	60	69	75	74	67	57	48	42
Sweden	rain	1.5	1	1	1	1.5	2	2.5	3	2.5	2	2	1.5
	temp.	26	26	30	40	50	59	63	61	53	44	36	32
Switzerland	rain	2.5	2	2	2	2.5	3.5	2.5	4	3	3	3.5	2
	temp.	34	35	43	50	57	63	68	66	60	50	42	35
Yugoslavia	rain	1.5	1	1.5	2	3	3	2	2	2	3	2	2
	temp.	33	39	43	53	62	71	70	71	64	49	41	36

Norway Almost all tourists visit Norway from mid-May to mid-September, to take advantage of the mild summer weather and long days of light. Dark and cold in the off season!

Portugal Very hot summers from late May to late August, ideal spring and fall weather (bright, dry, mild, breezy). Cool, windy, wet winters, with February the worst month.

Sardinia Basically a summer-oriented vacation spot, although pleasant in late spring and early fall as well.

Sicily Noted for excellent off-season weather. Many clear, warm winter days—not hot, however! Very hot in the summer. Nicest in spring and fall.

Spain Madrid is "nine months hell, three months winter," according to a Spanish saying. And so it can be cold and snowy in the highest capital of Europe. Best visited in late April, May, late Spetember, and October. The Costa del Sol offers mild winter weather, torrid summers—very popular with Scandinavians!

Sweden Visit from mid-May to early October to take advantage of long days and warm nights.

Switzerland Lovely from late April to early October. Cold and gray in the valleys during the winter—go to the ski resorts for sunshine. Most mountain resorts open winter and summer only, despite temperate spring and fall weather—which is ideal for visiting the major cities.

Yugoslavia The coastline, the major attraction of this country, should be visited in the summer—not only because the weather is best, but also because many hotels and restaurants close in the off season.

The Best of Europe

Andorra	A lovely isolated mountain retreat with superb duty-free shopping.
Austria	In **Vienna,** you'll want to see the Spanish Riding School (closed Monday and from mid-June to August), the Boys' Choir (9:30 a.m. Mass from mid-September to late June), the Hofburg (free Sunday), the Imperial Treasury (closed Friday), the Museum of Fine Arts, and Schoenbrunn Palace.
	In **Salzburg,** go to the Hellbrunn Palace and underground through the Hallein Salt Mine (hard hats and all).
	On a clear day, take the **Grossglockner** Mountain drive from Lienz to Zell am Zee. Bring enough Austrian currency to pay the toll and for gas.
	Seefeld (near **Innsbruck**) offers a lively casino and resort life.
	Skiing in the Austrian **Alps**—don't go at Christmas or Easter.
Azores	For total isolation and stark beauty. Go in July when the hydrangeas bloom.
Belgium	Fabulous food, from fresh mussels to Ardennes ham.
	In **Brussels,** visit the Grand' Place and Royal Palace.
	In **Antwerp,** you'll find Flemish masters in the Museum of Fine Arts. Take in the House of Rubens, several of his paintings in the Cathedral (they're covered until noon), and the Plantin House.
	In **Bruges,** hear carillon concerts at the Basilica of the Holy Blood on Wednesday and Saturday at 11:45 a.m. January to September. The world-famous Procession of the Holy Blood takes place in late May.
	In **Ghent,** visit the St. Bavon Cathedral.
	Outstanding are the castles of **Beloeil** and **Chimay** and the Château of **Annevoie-Rouillon.**
	Try to visit a rural inn in the **Ardennes** region.
	Binche's Carnival on Shrove Tuesday is one of the great festivals of Europe.
Canary Islands	These offer excellent off-season weather, low prices, and varied scenery from desert to tropical.
Corsica	Popular offbeat destination in summer with isolated bathing beaches. Rustic.
Crete	Forbidding and dry island famed for the ruins of **Knossos.** Good off-season weather from March to November and relatively low prices. Rustic.
Denmark	In **Copenhagen,** shop along the **Strøget,** go to the Tivoli Amusement Park (open May to mid-September and best at night), the Ny Carlsbery Glyptotek (impressionists; closed Monday), the Royal Theatre (September to May), Amalienborg Palace (Changing of the Guard at noon when the Queen is in residence), Rosenborg Castle, and the suburb of **Dragør.**
	In **Helsingør** you'll find Kronborg Castle.
	Stay in at least one country inn (**kro**).

Finland	Excellent trout fishing in summer.
France	**Paris**, with fabulous food, sightseeing, shopping, and sex. Here are the top ten sights followed by the most convenient Métro (subway) station:

Arc de Triomphe (Étoile)
Eiffel Tower (Trocadéro)
Invalides and Tomb of Napoleon (Invalides)
Louvre (Palais Royal—closed Tuesday)
Musée de Jeu de Paume (Concorde)
Notre Dame (Cité—10 a.m. mass)
Panthéon (St. Michel)
Sacré Coeur (Abbesses)
Sainte Chapelle (Cité)
Versailles (Pont de Sèvres, then bus 171)

The château country of the **Loire** with Son et Lumière shows from May to September. Don't miss **Chenonceaux.**
The **Riviera** (Côte d'Azur), best in spring and fall. Most lively in summer.
The cathedrals of **Amiens, Chartres,** and **Reims.**
The wine road from **Mâcon** to **Dijon.**
Mont St. Michel in Normandy.
The medieval city of **Carcassonne.**
Skiing in the French **Alps** (don't go at Christmas or Easter).
Prehistory of the area around **Les Eyzies-de-Tayac.**
Stays in château hotels and **relais de campagne** (country inns).

Germany	**Munich** offers both sightseeing and beer halls. The technical museum is outstanding, as is the Oktoberfest from late September to early October.

A trip through the **Black Forest** with stays in **Romantik Hotels.**
A trip along the **Rhine**, using Koblenz as a base.
Neuschwanstein Castle in the south.
The medieval towns of **Rothenburg ob der Tauber** and **Dinkelsbühl.**
The Richard Wagner Festival in **Bayreuth** from late May to September.
Sex and night life along **Hamburg**'s Reeperbahn.
A must—the cathedral of **Cologne** (Köln).
Stays in **castles** and **Romantik Hotels.**
The Wall in **Berlin.**

Gibraltar	The **Rock**, duty-free shopping for real bargains, and mild weather in spring and fall.
Great Britain	**London,** with terrific shopping, theater, and sightseeing. Here are the top eleven sights followed by the most convenient tube (subway) station:

British Museum, Great Russell Street (Holborn)
Buckingham Palace—Changing of the Guard at 11:30 a.m. (Victoria)
Houses of Parliament (Westminster)

Great Britain (continued)	Madam Tussaud's Waxworks, Marylebone Road (Baker Street) National Gallery (Trafalgar Square) National Portrait Gallery, St. Martin's Place (Trafalgar Square) St. Paul's Cathedral, Ludgate Hill (St. Paul's) Tate Gallery, Millbank (Pimlico) Tower of London (Tower Hill) Victoria and Albert Museum, Cromwell Road (South Kensington) Westminster Abbey (Westminster) Theater at **Stratford-upon-Avon** from May to January. Great cathedrals: **Canterbury, Chichester, Winchester, York**—to name a few. The well-preserved Roman baths at **Bath.** **Stonehenge** and **Hadrian's Wall** for lovers of ruins. Peter Scott's unique bird sanctuary at **Slimbridge.** The college towns of **Cambridge** and **Oxford.** Medieval gems like the town of **Chester.** Scenic tours through **Cornwall** (spring), **Dorset** (fall), and the **Lake Country** (summer). Stays in charming **historic inns.** Salmon fishing and upland game shooting in **Scotland.** **Edinburgh**'s Royal Mile.
Greece	**Athens**, with a visit to the Acropolis and the National Archaeological Museum (pay the extra fee for the Santorini exhibit). Make excursions to the temples at **Sounion** and **Delphi.** The **Greek Islands**—all fascinating. If you're short on time, go to those just off the coast. The monasteries of **Météora** and **Mt. Athos** (men only) for Byzantine art. Excellent weather from April to early November. Greek Orthodox Easter (different date than our Easter). Ruins in the **Peloponnesus**, the region southwest of Athens. Theater at **Epidauros** in summer (exceptional acoustics). **Dafni** wine festival from July to September. Excellent value for your travel dollar.
Iceland	Fascinating geology: volcanoes, glaciers, faults (visit **Eldga**). Lovely falls, including **Dettifoss** and **Gulfoss.** Trout and salmon fishing—the latter requiring advance preparation. Bird watching: **Eldey Rock** and **Thjorsarver.**
Ireland	In **Dublin,** visit the **Trinity College** library and see The Book of Kells. See the **National Museum** (closed Mondays), the lovely eighteenth-century architecture of **Merrion Square,** the **Abbey** and **Gaiety Theaters, St. Patrick's Cathedral** (where Jonathan Swift is buried), and the **GPO,** the headquarters of the 1916 Easter rebellion. You can shop along **Grafton Street.**

Ireland **(continued)**	Take a short trip south out of Dublin to the **Martello tower** in **Sandycove**, site of the James Joyce Museum. Make sure you visit the southwest of Ireland. Spend a day or two on the **Dingle Peninsula,** gazing out from **Slea Head** to the **Blasket Islands.** The **Cliffs of Moher** in **County Clare.** The **Aran Islands,** a three-hour boat trip out of **Galway.** Yeats country in **Sligo** in the northwest, including his famous burial site at Drumcliffe Churchyard under **Ben Bulben.** Beautiful **Donegal** in the northwest.
Italy	In **Florence**, a fabulous Renaissance city, visit the Academia (closed Monday) and the Baptistry. Duomo Medici Chapels Palazzo Vecchio Pitti Palace Ponte Vecchio Santa Maria del Fiore Uffizi Gallery **Milan,** famed for La Scala Opera from December to May. See its cathedral, the paintings by Leonardo da Vinci in the Pinacoteca Ambrosiana, and his "Last Supper" in Santa Maria delle Grazie (closed Monday). **Rome** is a must on any itinerary. While there, see: Colosseum (closed Sunday) Forum (closed Tuesday) Pantheon Trevi Fountain Vatican with St. Peter's Basilica In **Venice**, best visited in spring and late fall, see: Bridge of Sighs Doge's Palace Grand Canal San Marco Excellent and relatively inexpensive skiing in the Italian **Alps.** **Pompeii** (near Naples) and **Paestum**—some of the most fascinating ruins in Europe. Superb off-season weather in **Sicily.** Elegant summer resort area— the **Costa Smeralda** in **Sardinia.** Very expensive! The catacombs of **Naples.** Stunning drives: **Amalfi Drive**, a tour of the **Como Lake** region, the **Italian Riviera** from the border of France south. Famous festivals: the **Calcio** in **Florence** in June and the **Palio** in **Siena** in both July and August.
Liechtenstein	Famous for its colorful stamps.
Madeira	Lush island with good off-season weather. Swimming is in pools only: the shore is rocky, and off-shore currents are treacherous. Shopping for handmade lace, wicker items, and varieties of the excellent Madeira wines.

Majorca	Hot and dry summer weather with excellent bathing areas. Low off-season prices (winter weather mild but not warm).
Monaco	World-famous casino **Monte Carlo** and world's largest aquarium.
Netherlands	**Amsterdam:** sightseeing and sex. Best sights: Anne Frank's house Rembrandt's house Rijksmuseum Stedelijk museum Van Gogh museum And the red light district (fascinating and totally safe at night—with common sense and reasonable caution). **Keukenhof** (near **Lisse**) with fabulous beds of tulips in full bloom from mid-March to early April—only a forty-five-minute drive from Amsterdam. Twenty-one windmills spin on Saturdays in the summer at **Kinderdijk** (near **Rotterdam**). Take in **The Hague**'s Gemeentemuseum, Mauritshuis museum, and Maduradam (Holland in Miniature—open summers only). **Haarlem**'s Frans Hals Museum (check into candlelight music from April to August). The ancient villages of **Volendam** and **Monnickendam.** The cheese market at **Alkmaar** each Friday from 10:00 a.m. until noon from late April to late September (take the Kaas-Express train from the central railway station—much less expensive than most organized tour buses). **Aalsmeer**'s Flower Auction at 8:00 a.m. Monday to Saturday. See the reclamation project at the **Delta Expo** on the coast.
Norway	Visit the great fjords from May to September—**Geiranger** is one of the best! Take the train (**Bergensbanen**) from **Oslo** to **Bergen**—one of Europe's finest railway excursions. Also stunning: a coastal trip on the Bergen Line's mail boat—make reservations months in advance! **Pulpit Rock** east of **Stavanger.** The Munch and Viking Ship Museums in **Oslo.** The Midnight Sun from late May to late July at **Kirkenes** (far north). Try **Lake Svela** in mid-June for trout fishing. Superb cross-country skiing in March. The ancient cathedrals of **Stavanger** and **Trondheim.**
Portugal	Not to miss in **Lisbon:** Alfama (old Moorish quarter) Coach Museum (closed Monday) Madre de Deus church Mosteiro dos Jéronimos Torre de Belém Visit the hilltop town of **Sintra** (best in spring).

Portugal (continued)	Excellent weather and swimming on the southern coast **(Algarve)** from late March to early November. Base yourself in **Albufeira** (lively) or **Praia da Rocha** (cliffs over the sea). Don't miss the cathedrals of **Alcobaça** and **Batalha**. Incredible religious processions of **Fátima** on the eve of May 13 and October 13. Go to **Santarém** in June to see colorful bullfights. Great resorts with lively social scene: **Estoril** and **Cais-cais**. Ancient towns full of atmosphere: **Elvas, Estremoz, Évora, Obidos**. The Manueline architecture of **Tomar**, truly unique to Portugal. The fish market in **Sines** (go in the morning). **Coimbra**'s world-famous library. The colorful spectacle of fishing at **Nazaré**. Stays in **pousadas**, charming country inns. Port wine tasting in **Vila Nova de Gaia**, across the river from **Oporto**.
Rhodes	Mild off-season weather and fascinating architecture.
Sardinia	Luxury summer resorts on the **Costa Smeralda**—very fashionable and equally expensive. Good weather from April to October.
Sicily	Excellent off-season weather.
Spain	**Madrid**'s museums, with much time devoted to the Prado (closed Monday). An excursion to **Toledo** (give it a full day or more). Good swimming weather in resorts along the **Costa del Sol** from April to early November. Bullfighting in **Madrid** and **Barcelona**. Running of the Bulls in **Pamplona** in early June. The great tourist cities of **Córdoba, Granada** (The Alhambra), and **Seville** (Cathedral and Alcazar). Duck hunting near **Valencia** by advance arrangement. The ancient town of **Santiago do Compostela** in the northwest. Wine tasting in **Jérez de la Frontera** (go in September). **Las Fallas** celebration in **Valencia** on March 19. Tennis in **Fuengirola** (superb spring and fall). Stays in **paradores** (inexpensive country inns).
Sweden	**Stockholm** for Drottningholm Opera from May to September. Interesting Wasa Museum (sunken ship faithfully restored). The **Göta Canal** trip from Gothenburg to Stockholm, from mid-May through August. Reserve space weeks in advance. Midnight sun at **Luleå** from late May to mid-August. Salmon fishing at **Morrun** in mid-March.
Switzerland	A trip to **Zermatt** (the Matterhorn) or to the **Jungfrau**. Stays in medieval towns like **Gottlieben** (tiny) or **Stein-am-Rhein** (a gem).

Switzerland (continued)	Outstanding high-mountain skiing in the Swiss **Alps** (avoid Christmas and Easter). Stunning lake area in the south known as **Ticino** (go any time from late April to late October).
Yugoslavia	One of the world's great scenic drives along a stunning and varied coastline. Seven hundred offshore islands for romantic retreats. A stay in **Sveti Stephan.** A trip to the inland lakes of **Plitvicka Jezera.** A stay in **Dubrovnik** with plenty of time to walk. The mosques of **Banja Luka, Mostar,** and **Sarajevo** (take off your shoes).

Budget Planning Sheet

Before you make your final plans you should come up with an overall budget for your trip. It may be difficult for you to judge costs until you've finished reading this book and have looked at the sources of information I recommend, but at some point you should fill in your budget sheet with the most accurate figures you can find.

Item	Cost
Family, house, pet and plant care while you're gone..........................	_____
Documents and vaccinations..................	_____
Wardrobe and luggage......................	_____
Incidentals (film, gifts to take, etc.)............	_____
Transportation to and from airport............	_____
Transportation to and from Europe............	_____
Transportation within Europe.................	_____
Lodging....................................	_____
Food and Drink.............................	_____
Sightseeing and Entertainment...............	_____
Shopping	_____
Miscellaneous	_____
Emergency Fund...........................	_____
Total Cost	_____

INDEX

Boldface page numbers indicate material in maps and charts.

Free Things for Travelers

Dozens of other free things for travelers are described throughout this book. They'll save you hundreds of dollars if you'll make use of them, and so will these.

- Note that you can get a passport with more pages (and more room for visas, etc.) at no extra charge. It is ideal for extensive travel. Ask for it if you'll need it.

- Get traveler's checks free of any service charge from Deak & Co., 1800 K St. N.W., Washington, DC 20006 or Perera, 630 Fifth Ave., New York, NY 10020. For full information write either firm and include a stamped, self-addressed envelope for their response.

- Ask for the free timetable called "The Best Trains in Europe" if you buy a Eurailpass. You can get it from the French, German, Italian, and Swiss railroad offices, from your travel agent, or from William Brennan Associates, 51 Ridgefield Ave., Staten Island, NY 10304.

- Check with WATS information to see whether or not there's a toll-free number before calling an airline or company. Dial 1-800-555-1212.

- Pick up a telephone credit card for free from the telephone company. Use it to make calls home from Europe and avoid the surcharges in many hotels.

- Ask about special incentives when booking a seat. Many tourist offices and airlines offer "bonus coupons" to foreign travelers. Some of these programs can save you a hundred dollars or more!

- Find out whether the international airlines you fly on picks up the tab for a helicopter transfer from Newark or La Guardia if your connecting flight leaves from JFK. The best time to ask is when you're making reservations.

- Ask the airline you're flying on to book room reservations for you—many do so without charge. But ask as far in advance as possible.

- If you travel first class, you can get business cards made up for free in foreign languages. Tourist passengers pay only a nominal charge for such a service. Ask your airline whether this super bargain is available.

- If a plane's coach seats are filled, suggest to the airline clerk that you be placed in first class at no extra charge. Airlines "up-grade" passengers when economy class has been overbooked. If you're dressed well, it helps!

- If your flight arrives in a city too late to make a connection, you can get a night's lodging paid for by most airlines. But you have to ask for this bargain since the airline cannot advertise the service.

- Find out about the thousands of foreign-made items you can bring back into the U.S. duty-free. To learn which ones fall into this category write for "GSP and the Traveler," a publication of the U.S. Customs Service, Washington, DC 20229.